DON'T BANK ON IT

Also by Alix Granger

Trusts and Trust Companies in Canada

Don't Bank on It

ALIX GRANGER

1981

DOUBLEDAY CANADA LIMITED
TORONTO, ONTARIO

DOUBLEDAY & COMPANY, INC.
GARDEN CITY, NEW YORK

Diagrams on pages 171 and 179 are adapted with permission from Statistics Canada.

ISBN: 0-385-17648-1 (Hardcover)
ISBN: 0-385-17649-X (Paper)
Library of Congress Catalog Card Number 81–43003

ACKNOWLEDGMENT

The research for this book was assisted by a grant under the Explorations Program of the Canada Council.

CONTENTS

INTRODUCTION

The Canadian banking system, once thought to be the oldest vestige of tradition and respectability, today takes part in some of the most commercial, most dynamic advertising campaigning in the nation. Everywhere, slogans like "Will that be cash or Chargex?" have become banking vocabulary and we almost expect to be greeted with the soothing smile of Mary, or the cool approach of Anne Murray, every pay-day when we are asked to wait in line through a whole lunch hour to put money in the bank.

As with most heavily advertised products, the banking products are difficult to find through a blitz of brimming smiles, rousing songs, and tap-dancing tellers. Too many uneducated consumers cannot see through the maze of "extras" being offered to realize that banks, like many other businesses, often have their own interests ahead of the customer's. Almost any well-equipped bank manager can convince the most skeptical consumer that a "red convertible loan" or a "Gold Key Account" is the best deal in town— too often it resembles the proverbial taking of candy from an innocent child.

I was compelled to write this book about how the consumer can use the banking system more effectively by the
story of a young woman who went to a Vancouver bank
manager for a loan. She got away unhurt, but only because
she has far more financial sophistication than her casual
appearance leads one to believe. One person she fooled
was the bank manager.

She wanted to borrow $10,000 to finance a real estate
investment, and she offered more than ample security for
the loan from her large portfolio of blue-chip investments.
Actually she did not even need to borrow the money, but it
made sense from a tax-planning angle.

How did our banker greet this prime client? He welcomed her with open arms and larceny in his heart. He decided that she did not know a great deal about borrowing
money so he put her through the usual routine that is customary for the most impecunious, unsophisticated client.
Finally, out of the generosity of his heart, he offered her
one of his "red convertible" personal loans with an interest
rate of 17 percent, knowing perfectly well that this borrower qualified for a mortgage rate of 13¾ percent or even
a rate of 12 percent on a loan payable on demand. At this
high 17 percent rate, the loan he suggested would have
cost her $450 a year more than she should have paid.

Fortunately her investment advisor stepped in and made
sure that she got the lowest rate she was entitled to. This
woman is one of the fortunate people who can afford financial counselling, but what happens to those people who not
only cannot afford professional advice but need it far
more? They get fleeced all too often.

These days, you do not even need to enter the door of a
bank to get into serious trouble; you can get lost in a paper
trail or a computer network through some incredible case
of mistaken identity. This is what happened to Walter Stew-

art, the author of several books on Canadian politics and a columnist for F. P. Publications, after he received a threatening phone call from an agent working for Financial Collection Agencies. He was pursued and harassed for two months because another Walter Stewart owed $200 to a Royal Bank branch in Winnipeg. "Two months of letters, calls and complaints," according to Stewart, "failed to dislodge the collector from my trail. Finally the Royal Bank closed my file, not because it was satisfied that it had the wrong man, but because it couldn't prove I was the deadbeat in question."

Even then Stewart managed to get them off his tail only because he wrote up the problem in his newspaper columns and finally went to the head office of the Royal Bank to complain. Its president, Rowland Frazee, showed Stewart a letter from Gerald Stephens, executive vice-president of Financial Collection Agencies, admitting that not only was his company to blame but also that a less aggressive victim would have paid the debt just to get off the hook. As if that was not bad enough, Frazee also "acknowledged Canadians are moving inexorably into computerized banking, which is less personal, and just as subject to error as the present systems."[1]

To add to the confusion, the chartered banks, trust companies, and credit unions that make up the Canadian banking system are growing more and more alike as they develop into actual department stores of finance. How is the average consumer to tell them apart? How does the consumer know when he is being treated honestly and fairly? And where is the rapidly increasing impact of the banking system on everyone's life leading us?

One place it is clearly leading us is to an invasion of our privacy. The most blatant example of this was the unapologetic admission by the former chairman of the Royal Bank,

Earle McLaughlin, that the banks and the Canadian Bankers' Association (CBA) scan their records to find out where federal Members of Parliament do their banking. Then the banks instruct their branch managers to lobby the politicians for legislation favourable to the banks. Neither McLaughlin nor the Canadian Bankers' Association thought that using bank records in this way was an invasion of privacy. In fact McLaughlin added that bank managers regularly scan cheques to find potential customers and that he personally would have no twinges of remorse about using bank records for many other purposes. He actually told a reporter, "Suppose you wrote an article on banking that was not accurate. I would not hesitate to track you down and straighten you out."[2]

These words are from a man who held one of the most powerful positions in Canada as head of our largest bank as well as twenty-three directorships in companies with assets of about $23 billion. He and his ilk can take part in a monumental invasion of privacy and manipulation of bank customers simply because nearly everyone in Canada who participates in the economic life of our society has at least one bank account. Millions of citizens are left wide open to having every aspect of their financial life spied upon. And it is legal because there is no law in Canada that protects the privacy of this kind of information.

It is largely because of present abuses of banking power like this, and because of a genuine and considered concern that such abuses will be more frequent and more serious if present trends are allowed to continue, that I've written this book. The second main reason is simply that a well-informed consumer is an intelligent consumer. While the present system is not all bad, it has many faults. This book is designed to give the average Canadian consumer a clear understanding of how the banking system works in our country, and to provide practical advice for the day-to-day user of banking services.

Part One, "The Banking System," explains how the system works and criticizes its faults, inequities, and unfair advantages over the average person. Part Two, "The Consumer," is a chapter by chapter analysis of the specific services we receive from our banking institutions (loans, safety deposit boxes, credit cards, chequing and savings accounts, investment advice, etc.). This section contains useful advice that the consumer can use when he or she seeks one of these services. Part Three, "Banking in the Future," lets you in on what you can expect a few years down the road. There are a lot of people who are frightened by all the talk of a cashless society and the impersonal, computerized banking machines that they will have to learn how to use. They also wonder about their loss of privacy and the ways in which they can be manipulated, cajoled, or even coerced by the banking system and big government through the perfectly legal use of the huge data banks of information being stored up in the central computer networks. Where are the safeguards in this system, if there are any? These are serious concerns which no governmental body is addressing, and every consumer should be pushing the government to do so. I hope that this book will convince its readers of the urgent necessity for greater awareness, and stronger controls.

PART ONE

The Banking System

1

How the System Works

At the corner of Burrard and Melville streets in Vancouver the main branch of the Bank of Montreal announces in large posters that it is open at 8:00 A.M., and through its four glass sides you can see the line-up for tellers at 8:10. Next door, the Royal Trust lures customers by claiming, "It could be your turn to own a Mercedes-Benz 240D." Down the street, the Canadian Imperial Bank of Commerce discreetly advertises Chargex Visa and covers up its windows with curtains. Across the street National Trust offers "No-Charge Chequing" and, on another corner, the Bank of British Columbia touts its "Bonanza Account" and "Inflation Fighter Certificates."

Along Pender Street, you are invited to "Save at Yorkshire Trust," take out a 12 percent loan at Canada Trust, to buy shares in the British Columbia Resources Investment Corporation, and sign up for a 9½ percent "Special Savings Account" at Vancouver City Savings Credit Union. North West Trust offers "Guaranteed Investment Certificates" paying 9½ percent, and another branch of the

Commerce advertises Western Express Lottery tickets in its window.

At the corner of Howe Street and Pender Street, you are invited to "Sail into Summer and Save at the Guaranty Trust," get a "No Penalty—3 Year Term Mortgage" at the Crown Trust, and buy a waterfront lot on the Gulf Islands through the Montreal Trust. The Toronto-Dominion Bank at the end of the block has "No Penalty Chequing Service," while the Bank of Nova Scotia offers "Home Equity Loans."

Three short blocks and every kind of financial service, each with its special rate and gimmick. No wonder then that many consumers cannot tell a bank from a trust company or a credit union. These days they all offer chequing accounts, savings accounts, loans, and mortgages.

This was not always the case. Even ten years ago, banks were not big mortgage lenders, trust companies seldom made personal loans, and credit unions were close-knit organizations. Now they all aggressively compete in similar ways for the consumers' business, even though their legal identities still remain very distinct through various laws and regulations that compartmentalize the banking system.

Chartered Banks

The chartered banks offer a full range of banking services to customers:

- —chequing accounts
- —savings accounts
- —term deposits
- —secured loans for consumer purchases
- —unsecured loans for consumer purchases

—unsecured personal loans
—mortgages
—purchase and sale of securities and foreign exchange
—safety deposit and safekeeping facilities
—tax savings plans such as Registered Retirement Savings Plans (RRSPs) and Registered Home Ownership Savings Plans (RHOSPs)

Banks in Canada are called chartered banks because they were created by a charter passed by Parliament. This charter was reviewed every ten years when Parliament passed a new Bank Act. Sometimes decennial revision of the Act got hung up by wrangling and lengthy hearings and Parliament then had to pass interim legislation to keep the banks alive. This happened with the 1977 revision, which was delayed for several years. Under the new Bank Act, banks can be incorporated by letters patent at the sole discretion of the Minister of Finance.

The Bank Act states that chartered banks are the only financial institutions that can call themselves banks in Canada, except for savings banks in Quebec. This is the reason why investment dealers are not called investment bankers, as they would be in the United States. The Act also establishes that banks are controlled by the federal government and inspected by a federal Inspector General of Banks. Because of this, bankers believe that they do not have to obey provincial laws. This attitude has serious repercussions for the consumer because the federal government has emasculated the Department of Consumer and Corporate Affairs. This move shows little concern for the consumer, especially in the area of banking legislation.

It also leaves the provinces as the sole protectors of the consumer, except that solvency requirements are rigidly enforced by the federal government. Fortunately, some provinces have passed very constructive legislation and regulations. British Columbia, for example, has laws that forbid a bank from seizing the property securing a loan and then also suing for the unpaid balance. It has also pushed the banks to draft loan agreements that are easily understandable. The banks were incensed and refused to comply at first but some adroit pressure from the provincial government finally convinced them that it would be in their best interest to fall into line.

The banks are given certain specific powers in the Bank Act and these powers have been increased consistently with each new Act. The 1967 Act, in particular, brought so many formidable changes that it seemed to hand the banks the world on a silver platter.

Before 1967, the banks could borrow money in the form of chequing and savings accounts. This money was then loaned mainly to businesses, or used to buy securities. To a very limited extent, it was also loaned to individuals or to borrowers of National Housing Act mortgages. The difference between the money earned on loans, mortgages, and securities and the money paid out on savings accounts formed the basis for most of the banks' profits. The balance of their income was derived from payments for services such as safety deposit boxes, safekeeping of securities, and selling travellers cheques and money orders.

Then a whole new world of banking opened up when the 1967 Bank Act was passed. The banks were no longer held to a 6 percent ceiling on consumer loans (or a misleading version of it) so they plunged into consumer lending with such gusto that they almost destroyed the finance companies. Some of the restrictions on mortgage lending were also removed and the banks became big players in this market, moving in fiercely when it was to their advantage and then pulling out just as dramatically when they had better uses for their money.

Trust Companies

Fifteen years ago trust companies were the secluded haven of pompous men in pin-striped suits with gold watch chains who zealously hoarded the bonds and occasional stocks entrusted to their care for the support of widows and orphans. Conservation of capital and a small but steady income was their great concern. At least that was the impression they conveyed through their overwhelming aura of conservatism, caution, and respectability.

They also ran a banking business of sorts. Originally it was confined to savings accounts but gradually their chequing accounts gained acceptance. Investors could also buy term deposits and guaranteed investment certificates (savings certificates with terms of one to five years with a fixed rate of interest). The trust companies have pushed this banking side of their business more and more until today the average consumer can see little difference between a bank and a trust company. They cover the whole gamut from personal loans to chequing accounts.

The one area that the trust companies still have to themselves is the trust or fiduciary business. No other kind of company can act as a trustee, although lawyers and other individuals can and frequently do.

A trustee is a person or a corporation who accepts the duty of administering a trust. In many cases, this means that one person hands over his money, property, and investments to another person on the understanding that the person managing these things will do so conscientiously and within the provisions of the Trustee Act of the province where the trust was created. This places a great deal of responsibility on the trustee because he has complete control of the trust property, unlike investment counsellors or advisors, who have much more limited powers and have to meet much higher investment qualifications under government regulations. A more detailed description of the uses and perils of trusts can be found in my book *Trusts and Trust Companies in Canada: What You Need to Know to Avoid Getting Taken.*

The trustee business is huge. In 1980, trust companies administered over $65 billion in assets of various kinds. Part of this money was in the form of personal trusts, many of which were created by wills as testamentary trusts to handle estates. Trust companies also act as executors of estates to handle all the paperwork and problems of accounting for a person's possessions after death, paying any taxes that are due, and distributing bequests to beneficiaries.

On the corporate side of the trustee business, trust companies act as trustees and administrators for mutual funds, pension funds, RRSPs, and RHOSPs. They act as trustees for bondholders and as transfer agents and registrars for companies, to handle the distribution of bond or share certificates and the payment of corporate bond interest and dividends.

Most trust companies have subsidiaries which sell real estate and manage property. Being able to provide that type of service is often helpful in the management of estates and trust accounts when a person dies leaving a family home, real estate investments, or a small business.

A rapidly growing part of the trust business is the management of investments. Trust companies have always done this sort of thing for personal trusts and for people who want to leave their investments with a trust company for safekeeping and possibly investment counselling. Because these services were designed for people with large investment portfolios, the trust companies began offering investment services to the small investor in the form of mutual funds, which are invested in bonds, common shares, and mortgages.

This side of the business is controlled by the provinces because it comes under the legal powers granted them by the British North America Act. All provinces have passed legislation defining the duties and powers of a trustee and have officers who regulate the trust companies. Regrettably, the system is designed more to protect and enhance the trust companies than it is to protect the consumers. The root of the problem is the Trustee Acts, which spell out the powers of trustees in great detail but do not assign any powers to the beneficiaries of trusts or provide any satisfactory means for compensating them if the trustee mismanages the trust.

Credit Unions

Apart from the distinction that shares are sold to members, credit unions differ in essence from banks and trust companies more in their style of management than in the range of their services, which are very similar to those of other financial institutions. Credit unions provide:

—chequing accounts
—savings accounts
—term deposits
—the sale of shares to members
—RRSPs and RHOSPs
—personal loans
—mortgage loans

—real estate brokerage
—life insurance
—investment advice
—mutual funds

These financial organizations started out originally as self-help money centres to provide loans to their members more easily and cheaply than banks. Each member bought a share or shares in his credit union and usually left money on deposit in order to provide funds for loans required by other members.

The members of each credit union were united by a common bond. It could be an occupational grouping like fishermen, or workers in a factory. It could be a religious group, or people who lived in the same community.

There are still many of these small credit unions around but the trend now is for credit unions to merge into larger organizations to gain such efficiencies of size as professional management, computerized bookkeeping, and more financial stability. As a case in point, Vancouver City Savings has grown so large and comprehensive in its membership and services that it is outwardly almost indistinguishable from a bank. In 1980 it had assets of $1 billion, earned $1.2 million, and provided a full line of personal banking facilities to its members.

The credit union movement has flourished throughout Canada. From 1975 to 1980, membership grew by 30 percent to 9.7 million people. That represents more than 40 percent of the total Canadian population. About 5.1 million of these members are in Quebec, 1.9 million in Ontario, and 970,000 in British Columbia.

Credit unions, like trust companies, are not controlled by the federal government. They are regulated by provincial laws that vary from province to province. In general, though, all credit unions are allowed to make personal loans, mortgage loans, and loans to the self-employed, such as farmers and fishermen, and to small businesses. To get the money to loan out, the credit unions sell shares to members, take in deposits, and borrow from other places.

Credit unions have also formed other financial institutions to add to the facilities they can offer their members. These include life insurance companies, trust companies, mortgage financing companies, a chartered bank, and savings and loan associations.

The money that remains after paying operating expenses and interest on borrowed money is used partially as a reserve for bad debts and then allocated for rebates to borrowers, dividends to shareholders, and social purposes such as the education of members.

Most credit unions in each province are united through a central organization which provides many important services to the individual credit unions. The "centrals" clear cheques through the banking system, provide emergency funds and management assistance where necessary, invest surplus funds, train members and staff, lobby for legislation affecting credit unions, and organize new unions.

The provincial centrals are united at a higher level through the National Association of Credit Unions and the Canadian Cooperative Credit Society. The CCCS provides liquidity to the provincial centrals while the NACU is primarily a lobbying and educational organization.

Other Banking-type Institutions

The chartered banks, the trust companies, and the credit unions are by far the most important deposit institutions in Canada, but there are a few others that provide consumers

THE ASSETS OF THE CANADIAN BANKING SYSTEM

$ Millions	1980	1979	1978	1977	1976	1975
Chartered Banks	171,296	147,285	122,128	102,819	88,790	77,169
Trust Companies	38,968	33,373	27,906	23,203	18,335	14,604
Credit Unions	30,902	27,338	23,976	19,618	15,692	12,791
Total Assets	241,166	207,996	174,010	145,640	122,817	104,546

% Share						
Chartered Banks	71	71	70	71	72	74
Trust Companies	16	16	16	16	15	14
Credit Unions	13	13	14	13	13	12
Total	100	100	100	100	100	100

with some similar services. In Quebec, there is a savings bank called Montreal City and District Savings Bank. In Ontario, there are two branches of the Province of Ontario Savings Office and in Alberta, there are Alberta Treasury Branches. All these financial institutions provide a chequing and savings service to their customers.

Who is Getting the Lion's Share of the Business?

The chartered banks dwarf the trust companies and the credit unions. Their Canadian assets of $171 billion are 2.4 times the combined assets of the others. The banks also have huge foreign assets of $110 billion; thus their total assets are 4.0 times the combined assets of the trust companies and credit unions.

This appears to be a huge share of the banking market, but if one looks back over a forty-year period the banks have actually lost ground, especially to the credit unions. In 1940, credit unions had less than 1 percent of the assets of the banking system, trust companies had 8 percent, and the banks had a whopping 92 percent. Although they still

1974	1973	1972	1971	1970	1969	1968
68,481	56,455	46,650	39,958	33,616	31,000	28,940
12,443	10,509	8,601	7,470	6,564	5,771	4,980
10,315	8,814	7,040	5,532	4,570	4,103	3,758
91,239	75,778	62,291	52,960	44,750	40,874	37,678

75	74	75	75	75	76	77
14	14	14	14	15	14	13
11	12	11	11	10	10	10
100	100	100	100	100	100	100

Source: Statistics Canada, *Financial Institutions 61–006,* Bank of Canada Review.

grew at about the same rate as the economy, the banks gradually lost their market share over the succeeding years.

The most significant period for banks began with the change in the Bank Act in 1967. Though the banking system in total has grown 8.9 times since then, the Canadian assets of the banks increased only 6.8 times, while the trust companies have increased their assets 9.0 times and the credit unions, 9.1 times.

Although this dispersion of assets in the banking system may look good for the consumer, there is no reason to feel complacent. The power of a financial institution really depends on the total value of its assets, so it is important to look at the total assets of the banks, trust companies, and credit unions, not simply their assets in Canadian dollars.

A comparison on this basis shows that the banks have grown at about the same rate as the system because of the growth in their foreign assets.

It is also important to take a closer look at the changes in the different markets that the banking system serves, principally the markets for deposits that can be withdrawn on demand, savings deposits, consumer credit, and mortgages. This points up clearly the dominance of the banks.

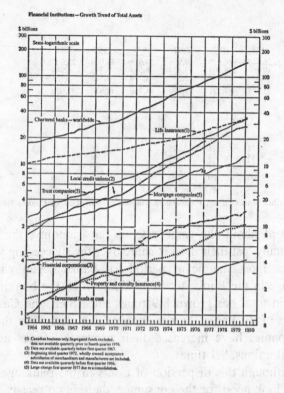

Financial Institutions—Growth Trend of Total Assets

They hold 66 percent of savings deposits, control 70 percent of demand deposits, and make 78 percent of personal loans. It is only in the mortgage market that there is an even split in the business. And control of these different aspects of the banking business is even more concentrated than these figures would indicate when it is considered that 87 percent of the assets of the Canadian banks is held by only five banks, the Royal, Montreal, Commerce, Nova Scotia, and the Toronto-Dominion and 65 percent of all trust company business is done by the four largest companies, the Royal, Victoria and Grey Trust, Canada Trust,

	1980	1967	Compound Annual Increase 1967–80
Chartered Banks	$281,244,000,000	$31,699,000,000	18.3%
Trust Companies	38,968,000,000	4,353,000,000	18.4
Credit Unions	30,902,000,000	3,382,000,000	18.6
	$351,114,000,000	$39,434,000,000	18.3%

and Canada Permanent. Concentration of economic power to this degree reduces meaningful competition and also creates a climate of superiority or disdain toward the average user of banking services.

2

Competition Versus Concentration

Canadians are overbanked. In fact, we have one of the highest ratios of banking branches to population in the world. The chartered banks have 7,457 branches, the trust companies have 1,083, and the credit unions have 4,528, a grand total of 13,068 branches of deposit institutions. That works out to one deposit institution for every 1,800 Canadians, including children.

Who needs that many branches? They add to the cost of providing banking services, and closing one-third of them would not harm consumers. But wait a minute. Doesn't a huge number of branches all fighting for business lead to lower prices and better service?

It should, but it does not in Canada for one simple reason. Look at the names of all these branches and you will find that 87 percent of the 7,457 branch offices of the chartered banks have one of five names—Royal, Montreal, Commerce, Nova Scotia, or Toronto-Dominion. That amounts to 50 percent of all banking-type offices. Clearly, the banking business is not a competitive business, no matter what the banks say.

How Do Banks Compete?

Competition works best for consumers when there are many companies of approximately equal size all fighting to provide the best product at the best price. Farmers can provide this kind of competition because there will be a lot of sellers of the same kind of vegetables, eggs, or chickens competing for the consumer dollar. So prices tend to be the same for the same kind of food.

Banks do not work this way in Canada because five of them dominate the business. This oligopoly, as economists call it, discourages competition and does not benefit the consumer.

Before the game was changed in 1967, banks just got together and set the terms and the public could be damned. Together they set the interest rates they would all pay on savings accounts. Together they set the interest rates they would all charge on loans. They all agreed to restrict the hours they would be open to the public and not to advertise on radio and TV.

The Bank Act of 1967 said that banks were no longer allowed to set interest rates in this way and a 1976 amendment to the Act said they could no longer conspire together to fix rates for services such as safety deposit boxes or chequing. This should have made banking more competitive but it did not, and any economist could have predicted that result. Companies that have a large share of the market are very adroit at finding ways to lessen competition, especially in consumer products and services.

A common tactic is to charge the same prices while getting consumers' minds off prices by emphasizing the services the different banks provide. Chequing charges may all be the same at the five banks, so emphasize the friendly smile of Mary at the Royal or multi-branch banking at the Montreal.

Another tactic is quite apparent in the interest rates paid on personal savings accounts. This is a game called "Follow the Price Leader." The Nova Scotia announces that it is increasing the interest rate from 9 percent to 9¼ percent. Within days, the others all follow suit and raise their rates to 9¼ percent. The banks have worked together for so long setting rates and general banking policies that they do not have to call a meeting to decide what they will charge on personal savings accounts. One bank makes an announcement and the others fall into place like dominoes. The only significant difference between the banks will be a few minor variations involving the amount of minimum deposit or the frequency with which interest is paid.

The interest rates charged on the typical unsecured personal loan change very seldom. In fact they increased only two times from 1967 to 1978. Then during the fast run up in interest rates in 1979 and early 1980, personal loan rates shot up. The fascinating thing that happened next was that other interest rates plummeted as fast as they had increased, but personal loan rates somehow stayed at their peak. After a lot of heavy criticism from opposition parties and consumer groups, the federal government chided them gently for this little omission and the rates came down.

Loans secured by investments are related to the "prime rate," the rate supposedly charged to the best customers. It is the same for all banks and fluctuates up and down with the rate set by the Bank of Canada for its loans.

There is little if any difference between these interest rates at the five big banks. The only new competitive advantage for the consumer is that banks no longer adhere to "no raiding" pacts that prevented a customer from shopping around for a loan. Consumers can now bargain for a better rate or a larger loan at different banking institutions.

How Many Companies Control the Banking Business in Canada?

Deposit institutions in Canada affect consumers in four principal markets. They provide deposit accounts, where money can be withdrawn on demand at any time by cheque or in person; and savings accounts, which legally can be withdrawn only if the bank is given notice; and they provide consumer loans and mortgages for consumers who want credit.

A study of concentrated market power in these four areas shows conclusively that the five largest banks in Canada dominate all but the mortgage market. It is no wonder that Parliament described them as the "major concentration of corporate power" in Canada.[1]

The Market for Demand or Chequing Deposits

The chartered banks monopolized this market from the beginning because originally they were the only deposit institutions offering bank accounts with chequing privileges. They still control the huge corporate accounts, but the credit unions have been taking a bigger and bigger slice of the market for personal chequing accounts.

DEMAND DEPOSIT MARKET

	Total Demand	% Issued by			
End of Year	Deposits ($ Million)	Five Largest Banks	All Banks	Trust Companies	Credit Unions
1967	7,455	80.8	87.0	7.7	5.3
1974	13,933	80.7	83.0	3.5	7.2
1980	24,328	70.0	76.1	6.1	17.8

Despite the inroads made by the credit unions, the percentage of chequing accounts held by the banks is still 77 percent, and 74 percent of these accounts are held by the five largest banks. That is concentration of a high degree. The hopeful aspect of this situation is that the proportion of demand deposits held by the credit unions more than tripled, from 5.3 percent in 1967 to 18.6 percent in 1978, probably because the credit unions have offered additional features. Some credit unions, for example, pay interest on chequing accounts, provide a line of credit, and allow their members to transfer funds from one account to another by telephone.

The Market for Savings Accounts

There has not been any significant change in the proportions of the savings account market carved out by the three different deposit institutions during the last four years. The banks did lose some ground after 1967 but the big five were able to hold on to 58 percent of the savings market.

SAVINGS DEPOSIT MARKET IN BANKING INSTITUTIONS

End of Year	Total Deposits ($ Million)	% Held by			
		Five Largest Banks	All Banks	Trust Companies	Credit Unions
1967	20,983	65.4	71.5	15.9	12.6
1974	60,379	59.8	68.0	18.1	13.9
1980	166,089	41.4	65.7	20.0	14.3

The Market for Consumer Credit

While banks and credit unions are the biggest consumer lenders, one may also borrow from sales finance and consumer loan companies like Beneficial Finance. Almost all department stores, car dealers, furniture stores, and many other merchants also provide credit for their customers. Policyholders may even borrow on whole life insurance policies from the insurance companies.

This market changed more than any other after 1967 because the banks were finally able to exploit their cheaper money to drive many other lenders into the tag ends of the market, the poor risks and the least desirable creditors. The banks carried out only 34.6 percent of consumer lending in 1967 but by the end of 1980, they had 67 percent, almost double their share of the market eleven years before. The credit unions had a small gain in their market share while the trust companies were almost insignificant. This may well change because they are now much more aggressive in seeking customers for their personal loans.

This huge increase in consumer credit provided by the banks was made at the expense of the sales finance and consumer loan companies whose proportion of the credit market fell from 27.9 percent to 6.4 percent. The retail stores also felt the pressure from the banks as their share of the business dropped from 7.2 percent to 3.4 percent.

CONSUMER CREDIT IN CANADA

| | | | | Compound Annual Rate |
| | Millions of Dollars | | | Increase |
Lenders	1970	1975	1980	1967–1980
Chartered Banks	4,663	13,149	28,095	19.7%
Quebec Savings Banks	22	58	166	22.4
Trust and Mortgage Loan Companies	—	199	1,474	—
Credit Unions	1,493	3,243	6,413	15.7
Total Banking Lenders	6,178	16,649	36,148	19.3%
Sales Finance and Consumer Loan Companies	2,851	3,054	2,703	—
Life Insurance Companies	759	1,149	1,781	8.9
Department Stores	720	1,232	1,429	7.1
Total Loans	10,508	22,084	42,061	14.9%

Competition in the Mortgage Market

The mortgage market is very different from the market for demand and savings accounts and consumer credit. To begin with, the trust companies and the mortage loan companies (which are often affiliated with them) have the biggest share of the market for mortgages. Secondly, the mortgage business is not particularly profitable at certain phases of the interest rate cycle and banks often choose to lend their money in other ways. Under these circumstances, the banks have tended to compete by rationing their mortgage money among their more favoured borrowers rather than raising mortgage rates, and over the last two years they have been gaining business by offering mortgages at lower rates, especially in smaller towns and rural areas.

MORTGAGES HELD BY DEPOSIT INSTITUTIONS

End of Year	Total Mortgages ($ Million)	% lent by				
		Chartered Banks	Trust Companies	Mortgage Loan Companies	Credit Unions	Quebec Savings Banks
1967	6,543	12.8	36.9	31.7	14.9	3.7
1974	24,863	24.2	35.6	22.2	16.2	1.8
1980	66,360	28.0	34.4	17.3	19.0	1.3

Closer study of the mortgage market shows that seven deposit institutions hold almost 50 percent of the mortgages in the banking system. They are Royal Trust, Canada Trust, Canada Permanent Mortgage (including Canada Permanent Trust), Canadian Imperial Bank of Commerce, Royal Bank, Bank of Montreal, Victoria and Grey Trust, and Guaranty Trust. This figure would be even higher if their share of the $9,899,000,000 of mortgages in estates, trusts, and agencies managed by trust companies were included.

Many aspects of the banking system in Canada are clearly concentrated in a few companies. This kind of economic structure is called an "oligopoly" by economists.

Michael Valpy, an associate editor of the Vancouver *Sun* said, "oligopoly sounds like something that lives in Lake Okanagan. It means, in the business world, the domination of a market by a few, and it is the label the Royal Commission on Corporate Concentration has applied to the Canadian chartered banks."[2]

As Valpy went on to point out the "heavy-handed domination by the chartered banks of Canadian business," the commission looked at the banks with such a jaundiced eye that they believed it was "desirable to promote by whatever means are practicable a greater ease of entry into the business of banking itself, and a greater degree of competition between other financial institutions and the banks."[3] A noble goal but a tough one to reach.

The banks naturally say it is ridiculous to believe the banking business is not competitive. They oppose measures in the Bank Act which are either designed to increase competition within the banking industry or to protect other industries being driven out of business by the banks.

Robert M. MacIntosh, executive vice-president of the Bank of Nova Scotia, got really wound up on this subject when he spoke to the Investment Dealers Association of Canada on October 17, 1978, on the subject of "Competition Policy and the New Bank Act," as follows:

> One of the biggest obstacles in the development of public policy towards competition among financial institutions is the lack of analytical clarity of the so-called experts who write in this field, especially academics. One of the favourite concepts that is used is that of "oligopoly," a word which most of the users cannot even spell, let alone define. In Canadian banking, what is nearly always meant by the word oligopoly is that there are five large banks which are said to represent 90 percent of the market.

But, as MacIntosh goes on to point out, the banks in total have "only" 71 percent of the combined assets of all the financial institutions in the banking system. That is not an oligopoly in the strict sense of the word even though it shows that the five largest banks have a very generous slice of the pie.

Much of the debate on the concentration of economic power really turns on how you define the market for a product. A consumer generally thinks of a market as a place where he can buy a particular product. Tangerines are not the same as oranges to people who want a fruit that can be peeled easily and pulled into segments without using a knife or getting juice all over the kids.

Most consumers do not lump all financial services together. They think of their bank accounts, their mortgages, and their loans as separate products, not as a combination of one large product, but only the most astute consumers will shop around for the best deal in each category of financial service. Mike Grenby, who writes a nationally syndicated column on personal finance, says he uses six different financial institutions.

It should be recognized that while many banking products are interchangeable, most of the time the consumer has a specific need for a fairly specific product. He needs a way to pay monthly bills; he needs a place to park savings for a short time and yet earn interest; he wants to buy a house, and he needs a car to get from the house to his job. It would be great if he could get these services at the best price from one place, but that is rarely the case. So the wisest thing he can do is think of each one of several different financial needs as a separate product and try to find the financial organization which provides the best deal. The concerned consumer should not consider all financial services he needs as one big lump to be taken as a whole.

Bankers look at the consumer differently because it is in their best interests to sell a package of banking services.

That is why banks offer package accounts and stress cross-selling of products in their marketing campaigns. The more they can tie the consumer into that one bank by providing for all his or her banking needs, the greater the profit potential for the bank. It is understandable, then, that since each bank wants customers for all of its services, bankers do not regard the banking business as a whole as lacking in competition. It is the opposite viewpoint to the consumer looking for a single service such as a mortgage and wondering why the rates are not more competitive.

How Should Competition Be Increased?

Consumers will never have the banking system they need until it is made genuinely competitive. Many government studies have recognized this ideal and suggested different ways to achieve it.

One of the most common recommendations involves measures to encourage the establishment of new banking institutions and to encourage smaller ones to grow to an adequate size. It has always been easy to start a credit union or a trust company, but it has been extremely difficult to reach the big leagues in the banking business.

In the past, anyone who wanted to start a bank had to put up $10,000,000 and then fight his way through a long process of getting Parliament to grant a charter. The big banks fought these new applications very hard and they were sometimes successful in preventing new charters. Mostly, this cumbersome process had the predictable effect of dissuading anyone from starting a new bank. That was all changed with the new Bank Act, as only $1,000,000 and incorporation by letters patent from the Minister of Finance is required now.

It is now almost as easy, in terms of initial cost, to start a bank as it is to start a trust company. In general this is a progressive move which encourages new blood. The disturbing aspects revolve around the solvency of these new institutions and the public's uncritical acceptance of a bank that can fail. There has not been a bank failure in Canada since the Home Bank fell in 1928—one reason why Canadians do not often question the financial basis for their banking system.

The fact is that getting started in the banking business is not that easy regardless of the initial cost. The established banks already have a huge network of branches all over the country in all the best locations. They have tall towers of glass and concrete in every major city to symbolize their power and presence. They occupy most of the choice ground floor locations of the best office buildings. This leaves little choice space for a new bank to move in.

Inside the glass towers, the big banks have accumulated expensive computer systems, credit card operations, international connections, and marketing organizations. A new bank would have to try to emulate many of these advantages at enormous cost.

All these barriers to the growth of new banks into the branch-banking business are so formidable that it is most unlikely that any new bank will challenge the big five in the foreseeable future. The existing smaller regional banks like the Bank of British Columbia or the National Bank just cannot hack it in the big league and have to be content with a small share of the market.

The history of Canadian banking is one of consolidation and merger into larger units which then expand through more and more branches. In the view of the Bank of Nova Scotia, "There is no doubt at all that if local and regional institutions had been well adapted to the conditions of Canadian life they would have survived, and the fact that they did not survive was an indicator of the needs of the country."[4]

The Bank of Nova Scotia admits that costs of producing a large branch network deter new banks, and only a huge organization can provide a wider variety of services, a large and profitable international business, and major computer capability. With these things, it is in a position to spread its costs over a much bigger base to achieve economies of scale. The only way a small bank can compete on these terms is to buy a service package of data processing and confine itself to a small geographic area or one aspect of the banking business.

This whole question of the optimum size for a banking institution is a controversial one. American studies indicate that very large banks are not more efficient than smaller banks. Canadian studies are not conclusive either way, unless you use one prepared by a large bank. Independent studies seem to run into a brick wall because they cannot get enough data to prove the best size of a banking institution that serves the general public. Even the federal Department of Consumer and Corporate Affairs has complained about the lack of cost data available to them.

Trust companies are also in a difficult position. Their traditional mortgage business will face more aggressive competition from the banks, while they still lack the legal powers to switch to personal loans on a large scale and have only small amounts of inexpensive demand accounts. This combination of factors makes the trust companies look longingly at the chartered banks and contemplate some form of corporate reorganization that would turn them into banks.

Several trust companies are actually planning to do this even though they face another problem—what happens to their trust business? Canadian tradition is firmly opposed to a bank being in the trust or fiduciary business because of the possible conflicts of interest that could arise. Trustees hold huge portfolios of securities in trust for individuals, pension funds, and charitable organizations. They have enormous powers to choose what companies to invest in, how to vote their shares, and whether to help finance companies by loaning money or buying new issues of their securities for their accounts. Think of the power that gives, let alone the potential power if they also did the banking business for these same companies.

American banks are in the trust business and that experience should convince any unbiased observer that Canadians should have no part of that practice. It has been strongly criticized by many people because of the way it concentrates economic power and the conflicts of interest it produces. This has led to a great deal of discussion in the United States about ways to split trust departments away from their banking interests and set them up on their own.

Continental Illinois was the lead banker for the Penn Central when it went bankrupt and it also held Penn Central stock in its trust accounts. Can a bank really give impartial advice to its trust accounts under these circumstances? Can it reveal private information without being guilty of using inside information?

An even more blatant case of conflict of interest occurred when the huge American department store chain W. T. Grant got in serious financial trouble. In a perceptive article, "Conflicts of Interest Within the Financial Firm: Regulatory Implications," Roy A. Schotland pointed out that "Connecticut Bank and Trust held so much stock in W. T. Grant, via family and family-related foundation trust accounts that, whether or not the trustee was in a 'control' position, it had unusual access to information. Rightly or wrongly, whether out of concern to abide by the law against misuse of such information or other concerns, substantial stock sales were made but were brought to a halt when the stock remaining in those CBT accounts totalled about $300 million in market value—at that moment. Not too long after the sales, of course, Grant went broke. Is CBT liable to those accounts now holding wallpaper?"[5]

In Canada there have been cases of trust departments holding large blocks of stock in a company which were crucial in swinging a take-over of that company by a corporation friendly to the trust company, or of trust departments holding onto blocks of stock as companies plunged into bankruptcy. The potential abuse is just too great to allow a bank and trust company to coexist, even if it does put the trust companies at a disadvantage in the competitive rat race.

Canada needs large banking institutions to compete effectively in the international market, and it also wants banks in small, remote communities. Consumers want a wide variety of banking services and they swamp the system with cheques which can only be handled cheaply and efficiently with a computerized banking system. We cannot have all those things without ensuring that the banks earn a reasonable amount of money on their investments. Recognizing this, the wise consumer should see that it is acceptable to give the banking system the power and financial stability to do the job but that it is also reasonable to expect that such power be balanced by an equal responsibility for consumer welfare. Consumers must be brought into the planning process. The old-boys network that holds the purse strings must be opened up. In the long run, this is the only way to fend off low competition and political pressure to nationalize banks.

3

Economic Power:
The Haves and the Have-Nots

Consumers have very little economic power. Small business is increasing in economic power. Large corporations and big unions have far more power. And sitting right on top of the pyramid are those faceless men who control the banking system of Canada, the three hundred directors of the chartered banks.

Peter Newman, in *The Canadian Establishment*, claims that the directors constitute "the most important economic elite in the country, placing the indelible mark of their personal interests, corporate loyalties, and philosophical predilections not only on bank policies but also on nearly every significant economic decision taken by the private sector. The bank boards distill power. Among them, the three hundred directors hold more than three thousand directorships of corporations with assets totalling $700 billion."[1]

These are the men who have the greatest economic power outside government in Canada because they make the decisions that really count in our economy. Their influence spreads into every recess of the country, building up the economy and creating prosperity and employment in one area, tearing down or restricting growth in others through their loan policies, their barriers to competition, their price-fixing, and their influence on legislation.

The board of directors of a bank exerts this power within the bank and outside it. Their first concern is to set policy and oversee management of their bank by approving large loans, examining credit policies, and encouraging steps to make the bank even more profitable. In this way, the board of directors can kill or create innovation, capital expansion, and jobs, depending on what and who they think worthy of support.

Many aggressive entrepreneurs were crucified by the banking hierarchy because they did not fit into a mould that the bankers could understand or because they might provide competition to an established company tied into the large banks.

Companies that already have secure lines of credit with banks work hard to develop a close relationship with the bank. First of all, they tie up a line of credit with a bank so that they will have money whenever they need it. Then they try to get their president elected to the board of directors of that bank. He will then be part of that cozy fellowship that looks after its own.

To many businessmen, this is the greatest achievement of their lives. In a study done by the Conference Board in Canada, an independent research institution specializing in scientific studies of management and economics, bank director after bank director reported this phenomenon. One of them said he "was brought up to regard it as the ultimate in prestige. I was so happy when I was asked to join the bank board that I darn near fell over."[2]

An outsider might find this hard to believe, especially when you look at the huge size of bank boards. In 1980, the five largest banks had boards with an average of 44 directors. The Montreal had 50 directors, the Commerce had 45, the Royal had 46, the Nova Scotia had 36 and the Toronto-Dominion had 41. This is three times as many directors as the average financial institution has.

The directors themselves admit that such large boards are not effective, for most directors cannot have any significant influence. The real decisions are taken by a smaller group of directors who then report to the full board for official approval.

Then why are all those directors there? From the bank's point of view, they are there to bring business to the bank. The Royal Commission on Corporate Concentration had some grave reservations about the prevalence of this practice.

> The nature and role of the boards of banks is traditional and certainly well known. The directors are, as far as we can judge, persons of ability and integrity. So we mean it as no personal reflection on incumbent bank directors when we express our concern about the situation where the boards of our major lending institutions are composed almost entirely of persons who have an additional relationship with the bank, usually as the chief officer of a borrower. Inevitably this creates the possibility of a conflict of interest, collective as well as individual, where the directors' obligations to the bank may clash with their duties elsewhere. Regardless of the degree of integrity and good faith that exists, in such a situation circumstances may cloud judgment. At present only a small number of directors on the boards of the major banks can look at and evaluate the policies, management and activities of the bank free of any complication that might arise from their own business connections.
>
> Given these circumstances, and recognizing the important role of the chartered banks in the Canadian economy, we rec-

ommend that the law require that a bank's board of directors
always include a reasonable proportion of members who have
no direct business relationships with the bank as borrowers or
advisors, or indirect relationships by being officers or members
of corporations or firms that are borrowers or advisors.[3]

The banks would be very unhappy if they were forced to
reduce the numbers of directors on their boards. There
would be many contenders for the remaining places at the
directors' table.

"It is the banks that run the private intelligence network," according to Newman.

[This] allows the men at the command posts of Canadian business to keep in touch [with each other]. The executive board
meetings of the five largest banks represent the greatest source
of non-governmental power in the country. During these delib-
erations are formed, strengthened, and multiplied the kinships
through which the Canadian establishment protects its existence and swells its authority. The corporations represented on
each bank's board of directors trace the bloodlines of big business in Canada. The clusters formed by this interlacing of
friendships, shared concerns, open doors and common policies
decide who gets what portion of the $40 billion in loans that
the banks have outstanding at any one time. The bankers' om-
nipotence is exercised through their ability to withhold favours,
to keep the interlopers they consider unsuitable from joining
not only their own clusters of influence but any other clusters
as well. This veto-power constitutes the chief element of the
bankers' might.[4]

Interlocking Directorates—The Old-boys Network

To be a director of a major bank is clearly to be a person with considerable power. But that is only the beginning. Most bank directors are also directors of other companies—life insurance companies, finance companies, large

industrial corporations, small companies, and private companies of all sizes. These interlocking directorates concentrate and intensify economic power much further. Sixty-three directors of the 5 largest banks sit on the boards of the 16 largest life insurance companies controlling 83 percent of that industry. The directors of the Royal Bank and the Bank of Montreal also sit on the boards of 44 percent of the companies which are among the 250 largest non-financial, non-banking companies in Canada. Eighteen out of 33 large insurance companies have 70 interlocks with 20 trust companies.

A report prepared in 1969 for the Department of Consumer and Corporate Affairs on interlocking directorates among the largest 260 corporations in Canada found that

> . . . a picture emerges of a rather complete interweaving of relationships among different financial groups. Table X indicates how the bank directors serve as official communications links between the other companies in the study. For example, the Bank of Montreal has interlocks with 73 other companies, and the Bank of Nova Scotia has interlocks with 38 companies. Thus any industrial company which has directors on both these bank boards, of which there are 22 such companies, has access to directors who sit on a total of 89 (73 + 38 − 22) other companies in Canada. That is 22 companies in Canada, by way of their interlocks with these two banks, have access to 89% of the 260 other companies included in the study, or 35.6% of the other companies investigated.[5]

Many commentators over the years have pointed out that interlocking directorships are a danger for a competitive economy. "One of the wonders of the world," in Allan Fotheringham's view, "is why the docile public of this complacent realm puts up with the unconscionable concentration of power among these few faceless men who combine all the worst characteristics of the civil service (humorless seniority) and the business community (arro-

TABLE X
TABLE OF BANK INTERLOCKS
(NO SUBSIDIARY RELATIONS INCLUDED)

Name	Number of Directors	Number of People Interlocked	Total Number of Interlocks	Total Number of Companies
Bank of Montreal	55	45	128	73
Bank of Nova Scotia	36	26	51	38
Banque Canadienne Nationale	22	8	22	19
Canadian Imperial Bank of Commerce	56	48	125	65
Mercantile Bank of Canada	16	8	15	13
La Banque Provinciale du Canada	19	10	13	11
Royal Bank of Canada	47	40	123	71
Toronto-Dominion Bank	36	30	80	51
Bank of British Columbia	15	3	3	3
La Banque Populaire	10	1	1	1
Totals	312	219	561	345

gance married with sanctimonious rectitude). Canada is controlled not by politicians, but by the system of interlocking directorships, with the banks the linchpin."[6]

The idea that interlocking directorates of financial institutions are against the public interest achieved prominence in 1913 when Louis D. Brandeis (later a justice of the United States Supreme Court) wrote a series of articles denouncing the practices and the social impact of the money trust.

> The practice of interlocking directorates is the root of many evils. Applied to rival corporations, it tends to suppression of competition and to violation of the Sherman Act. Applied to corporations which deal with each other, it tends to disloyalty and to violation of the fundamental law that no man can serve two masters. In either event, it tends to inefficiency; for it removes incentive and destroys soundness of judgment. It is

Industrial Companies		Trust Companies		Insurance Companies		Private Companies		Other Banks	
Number of Interlocks	Number of Companies	Number of Interlocks	Number of Companies	Number of Interlocks	Number of Companies	Number of Interlocks	Number of Companies	Number of Interlocks	Number of Companies
100	57	7	5	21	10	7	6	0	0
40	32	1	1	10	4	3	2	0	0
18	16	1	1	3	2	2	2	0	0
97	49	11	5	17	11	9	6	0	0
9	9	5	3	1	1	0	0	0	0
6	6	0	0	6	4	1	1	1	1
107	59	3	3	13	9	5	4	0	0
62	38	3	2	15	11	8	7	0	0
3	3	0	0	0	0	0	0	0	0
0	0	0	0	0	0	0	0	1	1
442	269	31	20	86	52	35	28	2	2

undemocratic, for it rejects the platform: A fair field and no favours—substituting the pull of privilege for the push of manhood. It is the most potent instrument of the Money Trust. Break the control so exercised by the investment bankers over railroads, public services and industrial corporations, over banks, life insurance and trust companies, and a long step will have been taken toward attainment of the new Freedom.[7]

Brandeis had good reasons for making these allegations against the pillars of the economic community. His views were based on a report of a special subcommittee of the Committee on Banking and Currency of the House of Representatives[8] and were fully corroborated by several subsequent governmental investigations on the economic problems created by interlocking directorates. These investigations led to legal prohibitions against many kinds of interlocks in the United States and much greater awareness of the dangers. Even stronger measures are advocated now.

A U. S. Senate committee recommended, in a searing indictment of the business establishment in April 1978, that interlocking directorates between all the largest corporations be prohibited; all types of interlocks should be prohibited between potential competitors and between a company and its suppliers, its customers and its sources of credit; a business "sunshine act" should be passed to open some corporate board meetings to the public; federal regulatory agencies should make public representation mandatory on the boards of large corporations; data on interlocking directorships should be made available to the public.

The study said the boardrooms of such major banks as Citibank, Chase, Manufacturers Hanover, Morgan, and of large insurers like Prudential, looked like virtual summits for leaders of American business. In addition, the largest commercial banks were too strongly represented on the major insurance boards as well as on the boards of major borrowers such as public utilities and airlines. These patterns of director interlocks, according to the study, implied an overwhelming potential for antitrust abuse and possibly conflicts that could affect competition, prices, and supply of goods and services.

There has always been one inevitable defect in these studies which allows the banks to escape criticism of interlocks. The Committee on the Judiciary of the House of Representatives brought it out during its investigation in 1965.

> Other investigations that have been undertaken from time to time have concentrated attention on the frequency and structure of interlocks, and not on behavioral effects of such interlocks. Accordingly, as of this time, there is virtually no factual analysis of how interlocking business organizations dealt with

past transactions and the social and economic impact of such transactions.

Without factual information concerning actual operations of interlocks, "commonsense" presupposition, reliance on past proofs, and abstract reasoning have been predominant in the analysis of both the virtues and the evils attributed to corporate interlocks.[9]

This criticism seems to fit most of the studies or analyses done in Canada on interlocking directorates. John Porter's *Vertical Mosaic* was probably the first widely read study of what he called our "economic elite." Its proof depended heavily on using numbers of interlocks but it did not delve into the way in which a background of certain schools, families, and inherited wealth produced the corporate elite of Canada. Being male, attending Upper Canada College, living in Rosedale, and having a wealthy father opened the doors to the boardroom. And once it was entered, many other boardroom doors opened and the old-boys network welcomed one of their own. This is really a sociological phenomenon, not strictly an economic one, so that economists have found it a difficult subject to handle.

The 1964 Royal Commission on Banking and Finance, as an example, did not add much significant information to the subject although its recommendations led to measures in the Bank Act forbidding interlocks between banks and trust companies and restricting the number of non-bank company directors who could be elected directors of a bank. The only justification for the second measure that the later Royal Commission on Corporate Concentration could find were "some general remarks by the Minister of Finance to the Senate Committee on Banking and Commerce about the desirability of less interlocking, spreading the distribution of the directorships and securing more variegated boards."[10]

In Canada no one has really come to grips with the question of how detrimental interlocking directorates can be and probably are. The concentration is much greater in Canada than it is in the United States. We have a small investor class whose growth is restricted by the elimination of common shares in mergers and take-overs, and the growing percentage of securities being absorbed by life insurance companies, pension funds, and other institutional investors. In addition, a large part of our productive resources are foreign-owned.

Another special characteristic of the Canadian economy is the close relationship between investors, directors, and managers. In the United States, the ownership of companies is far less concentrated than in Canada. John Kenneth Galbraith suggests that power in industry is passing from individuals to teams in a managerial revolution because of the need for specialized knowledge. He claims that the chairman of the board who has as his principal qualification his close liaison with the financial community is probably an anachronism. He is being replaced by men whose skills are related to organization, recruitment, information systems, and the prerequisites of effective group action.[11]

In Canada, we do not appear to have reached this stage in our economic development as yet, with the result that economic power basically still resides in the directors of an organization. A strong case can then be made to restrict the extent to which a director can abuse this power by serving simultaneously on the board of a bank and also on the board of an industrial or commercial organization, because the efficiency of our economic system relies to a great extent on the forces of competition to provide mobility of capital and ready access to financial service.

Many kinds of interlocking directorates are capable of

interfering with this competitive process. Since all financial institutions are competitors in one or more phases of their business, interlocking relations between companies in closely related fields may tend to forestall the development of competition. A bank director who is also a director of a company that leases cars is pulled two ways. He wants the leasing company to prosper while at the same time he has to support the bank's drive to get into the leasing business. The conflict becomes even more evident when one of the director's companies is a customer of the other. Take the case of consumer loan companies and banks. The loan companies need adequate lines of credit from the banks, especially at times when money is scarce. Should the bank continue to expand its own consumer loans, which takes business away from the loan companies, or should it use its scarce money to finance the loan companies?

The interlocking corporations also raise issues of abuse of insider knowledge in the capital market, the fiduciary responsibilities of directors of the companies they represent, division of loyalties, debasement of management through concentration of directorships, and the additional economic power attained by directors who are also able to influence government legislation through their positions as senators or members of parliament.

The relation between bank and insurance companies is particularly interesting because of the concentration of bank directors and the vast sums involved. A stunning example is Sun Life, with over $50 billion in insurance. In 1979 it had twenty directors, only seven of which were not also bank directors. Four were directors of the Royal Bank; four of the Montreal; four from the Commerce; one from the Banque Canadienne Nationale. In addition, three were directors of the Royal Trust, which is closely connected with the Bank of Montreal, and one was a director of Credit Foncier, a subsidiary of the Montreal City and District Savings Bank. The Sun Life also holds large blocks of stock in two major banks.

Friends in the Red Chamber

The Senate of Canada is another place that holds enormous potential for conflicts of interest. The Toronto *Globe and Mail* reported in July 1977 that "more than half of Canada's senators spend part of their time acting on boards of directors," including many on the influential Committee on Banking, Trade and Commerce.[12] Salter Hayden has been the chairman of this committee for twenty-seven years. He is also an honorary director of the Bank of Nova Scotia, yet apparently this poses no conflict of interest because he does not own any shares in the B.N.S. Senator Louis Beaubien was reported to be on the boards of five insurance companies and one trust company; Senator Hartland MacDougall was reported to have been vice-president and director of the Bank of Montreal; Senator Paul Desruisseaux was reported to have been director of the Royal Bank. Two other senators on the committee are directors of trust companies. These are men who investigate any legislation affecting our banking system and have a great deal of impact on how the Senate votes. What chance does the consumer have here?

With that sort of evidence, it is obvious that one group of people control a big chunk of the entire corporate assets of Canada. But is that necessarily bad if they are competent and fair?

In his testimony to a subcommittee investigating the Bank Act, in January 1979 Russell E. Harrison, chairman and chief executive officer of the Commerce, was incensed about proposed restrictions on bank directors.

"Speaking frankly, I find this provision a personal affront. Why should I as an executive officer of a bank be singled out this way? Each and every director of a public corporation faces potential conflict of interest situations periodically. It is a credit to our country that the directors of our corporations have conducted themselves so well. My definition of 'so well' is simply the rare abuse commands headlines."[13]

There is an answer to that. Quite likely it is only rarely that these abuses become public knowledge. They are kept very quiet in that closed society and only get revealed when they are too big to hide.

These directors seem incapable of understanding the value to the consumer of opening up the economic power structure to new faces and a wider outlook. As John Porter pointed out, they are in control and they jealously horde their power.

"They are the real planners of the economy and they resent bitterly the thought that anyone else would do this planning. Planning, co-ordinating, developing, taking up options, giving the shape to the economy and setting its pace, and creating the general climate within which the economic decisions are made constitute economic power in the broad sense. Nowhere is this power exercised more than in the small world of the economic elite."[14]

What Can the Consumer Do?

Consumers must support and advocate every step that is possible to break up this elite. Protests can lead to some positive action or a step in the right direction. Just look at what happened to poor old Earle McLaughlin, the chairman and president of the Royal Bank of Canada, when he told a bankers' meeting in Winnipeg in September 1976 that the Royal Bank was unable to find a woman that met the bank's qualifications for the board of directors. He said that simple housewives could represent women but could make no contribution towards the running of a bank. A storm of controversy broke out after this appalling remark and McLaughlin suddenly realized that not all women were housewives and there was at least one woman who met his qualifications. Mitzi Dobrin of Steinberg's was appointed to the board soon after as the token woman.

Consumers should also realize that laws and regulations are not enough. A law forbidding the director of a bank to sit on the board of a trust company may appear on the surface to prevent interlocking directorships among these financial "competitors," but there is a way around the law. It is that very convenient device, the indirect interlock, or the friend of a friend. Paul Desmarais, the chairman of Power Corporation, was asked about potential problems when Power Corporation's subsidiary, Laurentide Financial Corporation Limited, merged with Provincial Bank in 1979. Mr. Desmarais and several other Power Corporation directors are on the board of Montreal Trust because Power Corporation also owns 51 percent of that company. Therefore, they will have to resign from the board of the merged Laurentide-Provincial Bank organization.

Desmarais is not worried, though, about not being on the board of the bank. "It is pretty well run. Maybe we'll ask someone already on the board to look after our interests for us. Or we could have someone represent us who wasn't directly related to Power."[15] There is more than one way to skin a cat. Right, Mr. Desmarais?

4

Money and How to Manufacture It

The whole mystique about money may well be at the root of the power wielded by the banks. Few people realize the truth of the statement by an English economist, Sir John Hicks, that "Money is not a mechanism; it is an institution, one of the most remarkable of human institutions."[1]

Everybody talks about money but most people really do not know what it is in any precise way. In essence, money can be anything which is generally accepted in payment for goods and services. Beaver skins were a standard measure of value during the early history of Canada. Today we think of coins and bills as money, when actually bank deposits are the principal form of money.

The basic money supply in Canada on December 31, 1980, consisted of:

Coins and bills held by the public	$10,270,000,000
Currency and demand deposits held by the banks	$16,610,000,000
Other chequable deposits held by the banks	$ 8,119,000,000
Total Money Supply	$34,999,000,000

Canadians also had access to other money in the form of deposits with trust companies and credit unions which could be withdrawn on demand or transferred by cheque. These amounted to $5,777,000,000 at September 30, 1980. As far as the consumer is concerned, there is no difference between writing a cheque on a chequing account at a bank or one at a trust company or credit union. A more realistic definition of the money supply should therefore include all these chequing accounts, bringing the real money supply to a total of $40,776,000,000 at that time.

Until recently, governments have been unwilling to look at the money supply in this realistic way largely because they thought the deposits in trust companies and credit unions were of no great consequence. The banks had the lion's share of the business, and it was a lot simpler to stick to the traditional way of looking at money. The trust companies and credit unions were also content to keep the status quo because any real recognition of their part in determining the money supply would lead to greater government regulation and the necessity for them to hold cash reserves with the Bank of Canada.

What difference does it really make to the consumer how the government thinks of money supply? To answer that question it is necessary to explain why governments are concerned about changes in the money supply, no matter how it is defined.

It all started over 200 years ago when a political economist named David Hume ventured the idea that there was a direct relation between the quantity of money in an economy and the price level. Increase the money supply and you increase prices, according to his theory.

Since governments in effect controlled the amount of money in circulation, this would mean that governments had a major impact on the price level and therefore had the power to influence and direct the economy in many ways. But this power was not used to any great extent in the nineteenth century or early twentieth century because it was generally assumed that this was the best of all possible worlds and life would be much better if governments kept their sticky fingers out of the financial pot.

Then came the world-wide economic crises of the 1920s and 1930s and World War II. A new breed of economists caught the eyes of governments with their proposals to control the economic roller-coaster ride by manipulating the money supply. Control the amount of money in circulation and, as the economists advocated, you control inflation, unemployment, economic growth, and the international value of the dollar.

That was the start of thirty years of governments playing around with the money supply to further their political objectives of the moment. And to a large extent, the world seemed to work like the theory said it would. At least that is the conclusion reached by studying the results of a computer model of the gross national product built by the Conference Board to relate changes in the overall price level in the United States to changes in the rate of growth of the money supply. It showed that there did in fact seem to be a cause and effect relation in the 1960s and the early 1970s between increases in money and increases in prices.

However something went awry in the mid-1970s. Apparently people were whirling money around the economy

much faster than they had done before. The velocity of
money was increasing. Initially economists thought that
people kept the same amout of money on hand to pay for
their purchases and over a year this was a fairly constant
percentage of their total yearly expenditures. Then it became apparent that this was no longer the case. The velocity of money was speeding up rapidly towards the end of
the 1970s; this caused havoc with the price level.

Some economists and governments did not take the
trend very seriously at first. In their view, it was a miscal-
culation by the computer or it was a temporary aberration,
but wiser heads noticed something that they were overlooking.

At the same time as the money was changing hands
faster, the banking system was producing all sorts of new
substitutes for money: high interest savings accounts with
chequing privileges, cashable time deposits, daily interest
savings accounts, automated transfers between savings accounts and chequing accounts, telephone transfers, and
bank credit cards. Furthermore, consumers were finding in
many cases that a credit union or a trust company would
give them all the services they needed from a bank but with
lower interest rates for loans, more convenient hours, and
lower cost. The inevitable result was that consumers began
thinking of their own money supply in much wider terms
than just the cash in their pockets and their chequing account at a chartered bank. They thought of their money
supply as all the cash they could get easily, including savings accounts, term deposits, and Canada Savings Bonds.
The other side of this changing attitude towards money
was that the consumer began keeping a lot less money in
chequing accounts where it earned no interest. The end result was that chequing accounts grew much less rapidly
than savings accounts and term deposits, and banks grew

less rapidly than trust companies and credit unions. The whole thrust of the banking system changed rapidly.

As a sidelight on these monetary developments in the late 1970s, something else of a strange nature was going on. Substitutes for chequing accounts were growing rapidly but at the same time, the public was using a lot more dollar bills. In the face of all the predictions of a cashless society, an American study reported that the public is holding three and a half times more currency now than they held in 1960. These huge sums of cash are needed to support the subterranean economy of either crime-related income or people trying to evade high inflation and taxes by working for cash that cannot be traced by the government. The study estimated that $28.7 billion was held for these illegal purposes out of a total cash in circulation of $77.8 billion.[2]

The combined effect of all this money leaking away from the basic money supply and the control of government was to make much of the government's monetary policy either ineffective or at least much less effective. To understand this situation, it is necessary to look at the actual mechanics that the government uses to control the money supply.

How the Bank of Canada Operates

The initial way that the central bank in any country controls the amount of money in that country is to require all banks to put a specific percentage of their deposits in a special account in the central bank. In Canada, the Bank of Canada holds these cash reserves. The amount of reserves can change from time to time depending on the policy of the government as set out in the Bank Act.

The Bank of Canada can increase or decrease the size of

these reserves as it sees fit. Then the individual banks must make their own adjustments in line with the Bank of Canada's policy. If the Bank of Canada increases the cash reserves of the banks, the chartered banks can then take on more loans. This increases the money supply. If the Bank of Canada decreases the cash reserves of the banks, the banks must restrict their lending and the money supply falls.

There is one problem, though. This system works only if the government controls the total money supply. If money is escaping from the banks to unregulated deposits in other financial institutions it moves beyond the direct control of the government. It also introduces new characteristics to money. By increasing the competition for money, the banks and trust companies have made consumers more conscious of small changes in interest rates, less cheque money is required, and money moves faster and more frequently through the economy.

These economic changes mean that the government now has less control over the economy. Some economists therefore believe that the government should make all financial institutions subject to the same reserve requirements. Lacking this power, it is held, the central bank will not be able to induce changes in the financial markets to alter the price, terms, and availability of credit and so in turn to influence and control economic activity.

This viewpoint is not universal. Many economists and some Royal Commissions have thought differently. The Royal Commission on Banking and Finance in 1964 said, "Whatever the underlying pattern of competition, the effect of central bank action spreads through the whole financial system because of the competition in financial markets and does not depend on all institutions hoarding cash reserves with it."[3]

This conclusion does not mean that the Commission felt that there was no significant difference between money in the bank and "near-money" in the other financial institutions. They wished rather to emphasize that it is misleading to concentrate on the money supply instead of on the structure of interest rates, and to distinguish between financial institutions on the grounds that one creates money and the others merely mediate between savers and investors. The central bank, it is believed, can still control the growth of the money supply by controlling personal credit conditions, and hence there is no cause to extend cash reserves to non-bank institutions.

However, it has become increasingly apparent since 1967 that all deposits should be regulated equally. The credit unions in particular are increasing their share of demand deposits to the point where they are now significant factors in the monetary system and should be regulated on the same basis as the banks if monetary policy is to be effective.

In fairness, all deposit-taking institutions should be subject to cash reserve requirements—providing other relevant factors are the same. If the banks are given some special power which allows them to earn enough to compensate them for the disadvantages of operating under the reserve ratio, they have little to complain about. If trust companies and credit unions have fewer advantages than the banks they have to be compensated in some way—either through more lucrative avenues of business or through less punitive reserve requirements.

The original proposal by the government included the trust companies and the credit unions in these new requirements for cash reserve, but these financial institutions objected strongly because no interest is paid on the deposits with the Bank of Canada. Money that could otherwise be loaned out in mortgages at 13 percent must sit idly in the coffers of the central bank. The central bank in Australia does pay interest on cash reserves and the Federal Reserve Board in the United States has suggested to Congress that it should also do so.

The caisses populaires in Quebec also advanced the argument that a cash reserve requirement would place these provincial financial institutions under the control of the federal government. The federal government bowed to this political pressure, in the interest of either national unity or re-election, and exempted all non-bank financial institutions from cash reserve requirements.

Manufacturing Money in the Banking System

In early times, money was manufactured by making gold coins, catching fur-bearing animals, or stringing sea shells. Today we are slightly more sophisticated. Money is created within the banking system by making loans and buying securities. In technical terms the banking system monetizes debts, that is, it turns debts into money. At first this idea strikes most people as incredible. It appears contrary to the way we all look at our own finances. We use money to pay off debt. In other words, the consumer looks at the money-creating process from the opposite side.

To understand this, one has to look at his personal balance sheet and then compare it with that of a bank. Take the very simple case of Sarah Jones, who owns a $1,000 deposit in her savings account, a $2,000 Government of Canada Bond, and owes the bank $500 because she bought a preowned TR3.

Sarah Jones's assets are her savings account and her

bond, and her liability is her debt to the bank. Any money left over is net assets (assets minus liabilities), or equity. Accounting language expresses these ideas like this:

Balance Sheet of Sarah Jones

ASSETS		LIABILITIES	
Deposit	$1,000	Debt	$ 500
Bond	2,000	Equity	2,500
		TOTAL LIABILITIES	
TOTAL ASSETS	$3,000	AND EQUITY	$3,000

The bank looks at these assets and liabilities quite differently. The deposit is money that the bank owes to Sarah Jones while the debt represents money that the bank owns or has a claim on. Consequently its balance sheet will record these items on the opposite sides.

Sarah Jones's Bank

ASSETS	LIABILITIES
Sarah Jones's Loan $500	Sarah Jones's Deposit $1,000

One side of this balance sheet does not equal the other because the bank will be taking in deposits and making loans to many other people. When all these transactions are taken into account, the two sides must balance.

The bank's balance sheet will show on one side the cash it keeps on hand to meet the needs of its customers, the loans it has made, and the securities it has bought. On the other side, the liability side, it will show the deposits it is holding for these customers.

Sarah Jones's Bank

ASSETS		LIABILITIES	
Cash	$ 100,000	Deposits	$1,000,000
Securities	400,000		
Loans	500,000		
		TOTAL	
TOTAL ASSETS	$1,000,000	LIABILITIES	$1,000,000

This bank has taken in $1,000,000 in the form òf deposits, and for simplicity, assume these deposits are all chequing accounts. The bank knows that only a small percentage of these deposits, 10 percent, or $100,000, for example, will be withdrawn in the near future, so the bank keeps only that amount of $100,000 in cash. Banks try to keep their cash resources as low as possible because they do not earn anything on cash. They earn money by investing cash in investments and loans.

Sarah Jones's bank will consequently put the balance of the $1,000,000 into income-earning assets. In this example, $400,000 was used to buy securities, such as government bonds, corporation bonds, and other high-grade investments. The remaining $500,000 was loaned out to customers.

In actual practice, the bank's balance sheet will also have a section for the bank's equity, which represents the bank's accumulated ownership in its net assets. That part of the balance sheet has been left out to make the example easier to understand.

Now consider the effect of Sarah Jones's bank making a demand loan of $60,000 to Mr. Smith to buy shares in the B. C. Resources Investment Corporation. Mr. Smith will sign a form agreeing to pay the bank $60,000 within hours of the bank asking for its money back.

The bank makes the loan by placing $60,000 in Mr. Smith's chequing account. At the same time, it adds $60,000 to its loan portfolio.

Sarah Jones's Bank

ASSETS		LIABILITIES	
Cash	$ 100,000	Deposits ($1,000,000 + 60,000)	$1,060,000
Securities	400,000		
Loans ($500,000 + 60,000)	560,000		
		TOTAL	
TOTAL ASSETS	$1,060,000	LIABILITIES	$1,060,000

Recall that chequing accounts form part of the money supply and notice that this transaction has increased the size of those accounts. Making the loan has, in other words, increased the money supply by $60,000. In economists' jargon, the bank has monetized debt.

Note also that the actual amount of cash has not changed because Mr. Smith has paid the $60,000 to his investment dealer by cheque and the investment dealer deposits the cheque in the bank. This example assumes that both the investment dealer and Mr. Smith use the same bank, but the principle is the same even if they use different banks. Loaning money creates money in our banking system.

A bank can also increase the money supply by buying a bond from a customer. Sarah Jones's bank buys her $2,000 bond by increasing her bank deposit and increasing its investment portfolio.

Sarah Jones's Bank

ASSETS	LIABILITIES
Securities + $2,000	Deposits + $2,000

The bank has now increased the money supply by $2,000. This is a common way for the Government of Canada to change the money supply of Canada. If the government believes that there is too much money around, it sells bonds through the banking system and reduces bank deposits. If it believes that the economy needs a larger money supply, it buys bonds and increases bank deposits.

That is a simplified example of the way in which the money supply is expanded or contracted; in actual practice it is much more complicated. For example, money manufactured by one bank may be cancelled out by another if the money is used to buy another bond or pay off a loan at another bank.

How Credit Expansion Is Limited

There is a limit to the extent to which banks can create money. The government can place different reserve ratios on different types of deposits. One reserve ratio can be placed on deposits that can be withdrawn by cheque and another, lower, reserve ratio can be placed on deposits that can be withdrawn only in person or after a specified time.

If, for example, the banks had to keep a reserve ratio of only 5 percent on their savings accounts, these deposits could be expanded by 100/5 or 20 times for every added dollar, while a higher reserve ratio of 10 percent on chequing restricted the expansion of these deposits to 100/10 or 10 times. On the surface, this differential would seem to indicate that banks would prefer to expand by adding to their savings accounts, but remember that they have to pay interest on this money. Chequing accounts pay no interest but savings accounts do. If interest rates rise sharply, these deposits will become increasingly expensive for the banks and they will be less willing to expand them unless they can earn considerably more on loans and securities. This process places a real limitation on credit creation through the use of savings accounts.

Another complication to the ability of the banks to expand credit arises when the economy is depressed and the banks are unable to increase their loans in line with the increase in their cash reserves. During the depression of the 1930s the banks were in the strange position of having too much cash because most people and businesses who wanted to borrow money were poor credit risks. Companies were not expanding. People were not buying houses or cars to any great extent. The banks were trapped in a position of liquidity.

In the banking system as a whole, the government may request that the banks hold a fixed percentage of their deposits in the form of cash. If the legal minimum cash reserve ratio is 10 percent, the banking system will have to hold $1.00 in cash for every $10 in deposits. The banks will therefore expand their deposits only to the extent that they have this extra cash available in their reserves.

The mathematically inclined will realize that, in this case, deposits can expand by the reciprocal of the reserve ratio; that is, one over the reserve ratio. With a reserve ratio of 10 percent or 10/100, deposits can expand by 100/10, or 10 times.

Assume the cash reserves of the banking system are $350,000,000 and the reserve ratio is 10 percent. The total allowable deposits in the banking system will be:

$$\$350,000,000 \times \frac{100}{10} = \$3,500,000,000$$

If the central bank raises the reserve ratio to 15 percent, or 15/100, the effect on the banking system is dramatic. The new maximum size of the banking system is cut to:

$$\$350,000,000 \times \frac{100}{15} = \$2,333,333,333$$

This would mean a reduction in the maximum size of the banking system of 33 percent, or about $1.2 billion. This would be very deflationary. Conversely, a reduction in the reserve ratio can be very inflationary because it allows the money supply to expand.

A complication to the ability of the banks to expand credit arises when one considers the impact of financial institutions such as credit unions that have no legal reserve requirements. If the public takes money out of a bank and deposits it in a chequing account at a credit union, they are probably causing credit expansion in the economy. The credit union can use the money to make loans or mortgages to its customers to a greater extent than a bank can with the equivalent amount of money because it does not have to hold a legal cash reserve. It only needs to hold a small percentage for customers who may want to withdraw cash. The only effective limitation on credit creation by the credit union is its ability to earn money on its deposits, as some badly managed credit unions have found out to their sorrow. A credit union must be able to invest its depositors'

money in loans that yield more than it costs the credit
union to extend that credit. Paying too high a note on depositors' money or making bad loans brings an abrupt
halt to their credit creation.

Cheque Clearing in the Banking System

According to the *Globe and Mail,* Canadians' love affair
with cheques is going strong.

> The fascination Canadians have with the cheque as a pay-
> ments instrument continues to grow year by year as the total
> value of cheques written becomes staggering.
>
> On average, the number of cheques written on Canadian
> bank accounts has risen 3 to 4 per cent a year over the past
> four years bringing the number of cheques and other bank
> payment instruments like bank drafts written to about an
> annual 1.6 billion.[4]

In 1980 the total value of cheques cashed in fifty selected
centres across Canada was $5.3 trillion, up from $3.9 tril-
lion the previous year and $2.1 trillion in 1975. This
cheque cashing figure of $5.3 trillion is large by any meas-
ure and Canadians appear to use cheques more than any
other nation besides the United States. About 85 percent
of financial transactions in Canada are settled by cheque.

Cheque clearing has consequently become a major factor
in the Canadian banking system. It is extremely costly in
total and has become increasingly complicated as the financial system expands and diversifies.

The more financial institutions that are offering chequing
facilities, the more ways there are for a cheque to be routed
through the system. In the simplest form, the customer and
the store both have their accounts in the same branch of
the same bank. The customer's cheque is deposited in the
same bank it was drawn on. The situation becomes slightly

more complex if the customer and the store have their accounts in different branches of the same bank, because then the cheque has to be cleared from one branch to another.

An extreme example is a customer with an account in a trust company in the Yukon paying a bill to a friend in Yarmouth, Nova Scotia, who has an account in a credit union. The cheque is deposited in the credit union, passed to a bank in Yarmouth, then to a clearing centre in Halifax, on to a clearing centre in Vancouver, off to a bank in the Yukon, and finally back to the trust company in the Yukon.

There are nine of these clearing-house centres in Canada through which cheques are passed. They are funded by the chartered banks through their organization, the Canadian Bankers' Association. The banks charge trust companies and credit unions for providing this service for their cheques.

The clearing system was originally designed to handle only cheques written by customers of banks but the chequing business of the trust companies and credit unions has grown so much in the last ten years that these financial institutions wanted to join the clearing system, mainly to cut the costs of their cheque-clearing.

The government proposed changing this clearing system by setting up the Canadian Payments Association to replace the old cheque-clearing system. The banks, the trust companies, and the credit unions would all be members of the Association thereby taking another step towards unifying the banking system and bringing all financial institutions under federal control and direction.

Three important points emerge from the description of the workings of the Canadian banking system. The first is that the creation of deposits and the creation of credit are intimately connected. The second is that, given the requirement that banks must operate under legal reserve ratios, all deposit institutions should be treated equally. Thirdly, the cheque-clearing system needs revision in the interests of both fairness and efficiency.

5

How to Produce Profits
in a Bank

All banking institutions operate on three basic principles—
leverage, a spread of interest rates between assets and their
liabilities, and matching the maturities of assets and liabilities. If you understand that, you can follow the rest. It explains why financial institutions can be enormously profitable. It explains why they pay 6 percent a year on savings
accounts and they charge 12 percent on personal loans.
And it explains why trust companies like to sell you those
guaranteed investment certificates (GICs) that you cannot
get your money out of for five years.

Leverage

Anybody who has watched a seesaw knows instinctively
how leverage works. Two kids who weigh the same can
balance the bar evenly because the pivot is at an equal dis-

tance from both kids. Move the pivot away from one youngster and she will be able to lift a full grown man several times her weight.

That is the way a financial institution works. It first raises capital by the sale of shares to investors and then takes up to twenty times that amount in the form of deposits from its customers. The more aggressive a company, the more likely it is to lever its shareholders' investment to the greatest possible degree.

All companies start out by selling common shares, usually for cash. The balance sheet of a newly incorporated trust company might look like this:

ASSETS		LIABILITIES	
Cash	$1,000,000	Liabilities	$ 0
		Shareholders' Equity (1,000,000 shares at $1.00 a share)	1,000,000
		TOTAL LIABILITIES	
TOTAL ASSETS	$1,000,000	AND EQUITY	$1,000,000

The trust company would then bring in deposits and use these to make loans and investments. Using the principle of leverage, it can employ its $1,000,000 in equity to take in a legal maximum of $20,000,000 in deposits. Assuming it holds 10 percent of its assets in the form of cash, the trust company can loan out 90 percent of its $21,000,000 in assets, or $18,900,000. Its balance sheet will now take this form:

ASSETS		LIABILITIES	
Cash	$ 2,100,000	Deposits	$20,000,000
		Shareholders'	
Loans	18,900,000	Equity	1,000,000
		TOTAL LIABILITIES	
TOTAL ASSETS	$21,000,000	AND EQUITY	$21,000,000

All financial institutions operate on this principle of leverage. The more conservative ones will have a low leverage because there is less risk. The more aggressive ones will have a high leverage because that is the way to make higher profits—providing their borrowers are creditworthy.

The Spread of Interest Rates Between Assets and Liabilities

Financial institutions are often described as financial intermediaries because their main function is to accept money in one form and pass it on in another. A trust company borrows money from the public in the form of deposits and guaranteed investment certificates and then loans this money out in the form of mortgages. The purpose of this activity naturally is to make money. They do that by paying a lower rate to borrow the money and charging a higher rate to loan it. If savings accounts pay 9 percent and mortgages cost 12 percent, the 3 percent interest spread remains with the trust company to pay their costs of operation and to provide a profit.

The sound management of a financial institution requires that this spread between the cost of money on liabilities and the rate of money earned on assets is watched very carefully. At certain times the cost of money can rise faster than it can be earned, and profits get squeezed. At other times the cost of money may fall rapidly, and profits are increased.

Matching the Maturities of Assets and Liabilities

The third basic principle for operating a successful financial institution has sometimes been overlooked by managers of banks or trust companies, with disastrous results.

The chronic problem of all financial institutions is matching the maturity dates of their assets with the maturity dates of their liabilities. "Borrowing short while lending long" is the banker's definition of a ride on the *Titanic*.

Here is how this mismatch works to sink a financial institution. A bank borrows money from the public by offering them chequing accounts that can be withdrawn at any time. Then it invests this money in mortgages that are repaid over a five-year term. A rumor spreads around the community that the bank is in serious financial trouble and may collapse. The owners of the chequing accounts rush to the bank to withdraw their money, but the bank just does not have the money available for its depositors to withdraw in cash or by cheque. The money is tied up in mortgages, which cannot be sold and converted into cash quickly or easily. The bank has borrowed money on a short term, or demand basis, while lending it out for a long term.

The more common problem in recent years for many Canadian companies has involved the matching of interest rates. A trust company borrows money in the form of guaranteed investment certificates and savings accounts, and it must keep on raising the interest rates it pays on new GICs and on savings accounts as interest rates rise in the economy in order to stay competitive with other financial institutions. If the trust company does not raise its interest rates when other banking institutions are raising their rates, savers will transfer their money to the more competitive companies. But at the same time as the cost of their borrowed money is rising, the trust company has a backlog of mortgages at lower rates on their books and is having difficulty investing in new mortgages at rates that will cover the cost of borrowing. The result is the classic squeeze between the cost of money and the return on money, which caused severe profit declines in many trust companies in 1980.

From these examples, it is clear that liquidity and term are the most important factors in matching maturity. Liquidity is the ability of an investment to be converted into cash at a moment's notice without the investment losing any of its value from the transaction. Chequing accounts are instant cash in most cases, and it costs very little, if anything, to cash a cheque. Canada Savings Bonds can be sold easily on any business day and the owner can always get back as much as was paid for them. That is a very high degree of liquidity.

At the other end of the liquidity spectrum is a guaranteed investment certificate sold by a trust company. In most cases, it cannot be sold and cannot be turned into cash unless the holder dies. That is a stiff price to pay for liquidity. Trust companies love GICs because their lack of liquidity is similar to the low liquidity of mortgages, where the money from GICs is invested.

Between these two extremes there is a range of investments with different degrees of liquidity. Term deposits can be turned into cash if the buyer is willing to accept a lower rate of interest. Most stocks and bonds can be sold easily, and payment will be received in about seven days. Mortgages are seldom sold but are gradually turned into cash as the monthly payments reduce the principal value.

The other important factor is the length of time before the principal value of an investment is repaid by the borrower. In 1980 a Canada Savings Bond which matures in 1984 has a term of four years because the Canadian government must pay back the principal or face amount of the bond at that time.

Liquidity and term are important to a financial institution because it must invest borrowed funds profitably and yet stand ready to repay the borrowed funds when necessary. Ideally, therefore, a trust company will borrow funds from people by selling GICs that mature in, say, five years, and then invest the money in mortgages that mature at the same time. Both the funds borrowed and the funds loaned have low liquidity and a five-year term. A perfect match.

Producing Profits

A financial institution produces profits by:

1. Selling shares and attracting as many low cost deposits as possible.
2. Lending this money at the highest rates possible without taking on too much risk or without tying up these funds for too long.
3. Avoiding a cash run on the bank by depositors at a time when money is tied up in long-term loans.

If you analyze these three different points, you will realize that the chartered banks and the credit unions have an advantage over the trust companies because their money supply is cheaper. Trust companies raise most of their money through personal savings accounts and guaranteed investment certificates and invest this money in mortgages. In the summer of 1979, they had to pay 9 to 9½ percent on savings accounts and 10 to 10½ percent on GICs, but they could only get 11 percent on their mortgages. This is far too narrow a spread between the cost of money and the return on money to generate reasonable profits.

The credit unions are in a better position. About one-quarter of their deposits are low-cost demand deposits and they do a large business in loans which yield at least 12 percent.

The chartered banks have the biggest advantage of all. They have large holdings of demand deposits, and they raise substantial additional amounts on short-term deposits. These give the banks what has been described as a unique advantage, "a sort of built-in stabilizer which produces profits in good times or bad."[1]

When interest rates are low, the banks make good profits because they are borrowing cheaply and lending the money out at rates which often fall very little, if at all. When interest rates rise and the economy is booming, the banks make good profits because the volume of their business expands at a rapid rate.

There has been a great deal of criticism of bank profits, some of it deserved but much of it ill-informed. The Economic Council of Canada published a study that appeared to show that banks were far more profitable in Canada than they are in the United States. The trouble with this kind of comparison is that one is comparing the proverbial apples and oranges. The American banking system differs greatly from the Canadian banking system and figures have to be adjusted to such a degree that the exercise becomes almost meaningless.

A more reasonable approach is to apply some of the

basic principles of investment analysis to the profitability of Canadian banking. One test would be to consider the percentage that is earned on the shareholders' investment. In 1980 it averaged 16.2 percent. This is a good rate of profit by anyone's standard, but some other industries earn even more.

In economic theory, there are two types of profits. Profits over a long period of time are a return to investors to encourage them to place their scarce savings with that company, and their savings must receive a competitive rate of return or investors will move their money to other more profitable companies. Over a shorter period of time, some companies will also receive a premium profit because they have been more innovative than other companies and these short-term extra profits are an incentive for a superior company to encourage innovation. Without this extra incentive, economic theory says we would not have innovative companies.

If you apply this theory to the banking system, and compare the rates of return in different industries and factor in the tremendous demands placed on the banking system to develop new products for consumers or new ways of providing services to consumers, you should realize that the banking system must generate an adequate level of profits. That statement applies whether the banking system is owned by the government or by private investors.

From the consumer's point of view, the real issue is whether these profits are sufficient to promote the banking system the consumer wants and whether these profits are used in a productive manner. Are they being used to entrench economic power and generate a "consumer be damned" attitude or are they being used to deliver more efficient banking services? The jury is still out on that decision.

6

The Structure of
Interest Rates

Interest rates are an intriguing subject because there seems to be no end to their complexity. Economists have countless theories about why they fluctuate. Governments have all sorts of reasons why they should or should not fluctuate. Investment analysts have wildly differing theories about where interest rates are going next. According to the American Bankers' Association, there are fifty-four different methods of computing interest in common use. One expert even claims there are over a hundred. Under these circumstances it is easy to understand why the consumer can become confused over the terms of his loan, mortgage, savings account, RRSP, or RHOSP.

The rate of interest is basically the price paid for the use of a sum of money for a certain period of time. In general, the rate should be lower if the money is lent for a shorter period of time, providing the borrower is a good credit risk and the lender can get the money back at any time without paying an unreasonable penalty. The three factors affecting the rate of interest paid under identical economic conditions are then:

1.—term—the length of time until the loan matures and the principal is repaid.
2.—risk—the chance that the borrower will not be able to repay the loan.
3.—liquidity—the ease and speed with which the loan can be turned into cash without losing its value.

These three factors help to explain why different rates of interest are charged on different types of loans or are paid on different savings mediums. A combination of term, risk, and liquidity results in a structure of interest rates ranging from the least risky to the most risky.

A sample structure of interest rates showed this range of returns in the summer of 1979. The rates at the same time in 1978 are also shown to indicate how the whole structure of interest rates shifts when interest rates rise in the economy as a whole. Some rates, on savings accounts, for example, rise a great deal but other rates, on mortgages, say, rise much less.

	On May 8, 1981	On May 8, 1980
Low Risk:		
Bank savings accounts	14.75%	12.5%
Bank term deposits (90 days)	14.75–15.25	13.75–14.5
Medium Risk:		
Investment certificates (5 years)	14.5–15.75	11.5–13.5
Corporate bonds due in 20 years	16.24	12.24
First mortgages	17	14.5–16
Bank prime rate	19.5	15.25–15.75
High Risk:		
Second mortgages	14–18	14–18

Interest Rates and Inflation

The interest rate on any security is not really just one rate. It is a combination of several different interest rates added together. Each one of these separate interest rates is supposed to compensate the investor in some way for giving up the use of his cash. First, there is a rate that economists call the pure interest rate because it provides the lender with the income he should receive on an investment that has no risk. This rate is believed to be about 3 to 4 percent. Then there is a certain percentage to compensate the investor for the risk in loaning his money. The riskier the investment, the higher the additional percentage that should be paid to the lender. Finally, a lender should be compensated for inflation because a dollar tomorrow is worth less than a dollar today. If the inflation rate is expected to be, say, 8 percent per year for the next ten years, the investor loaning money for ten years will want an extra 8 percent added to the interest each year to maintain his purchasing power until he gets the money back.

Given these considerations, interest rates in a period of 8 percent annual inflation would be:

	Pure Rate	Risk Rate	Inflation Rate	Total Rate
Canada Savings Bond	4%	0%	8%	12%
20-Year Corporation Bond	4	2	8	14
Second Mortgage	4	6	8	18

But, in fact, lenders are not always compensated adequately for inflation. Inflation was rising at a rate of 10.4 percent in June 1979 while at the same time the Government of Canada was selling 23-year bonds yielding 9.98 percent. That rate made sense only if inflation dropped sharply throughout most of the term of the bond. Should it remain at the then current rate, the investor would not be compensated for inflation and would receive a negative real income on his investment.

As Toronto *Globe and Mail* columnist Hugh Anderson said:

> Investing these days, for professionals and amateurs alike, has become principally a question of beating inflation, rather than beating the market. If you buy Government bonds at 10 percent when inflation is 9 percent, you are ahead of the game. If you buy the bonds at 9 percent when prices are rising at 10 percent, you are a loser.
>
> Moreover, at a 9 percent inflation rate, the purchasing power of a dollar declines to about 50 cents in the short space of eight years.[1]

The Real World of Interest Rates

In the economist's dream of the perfectly competitive market, interest rates do reflect the differences in their term, risk, and liquidity quite precisely. But the market for money is not perfectly competitive and interest rates for particular securities or loans reflect this.

Aberrations in the normal structure of interest rates creep in as a result of government intervention, rates administered by the financial institutions, and cultural factors. Sometimes these controlled rates are beneficial to consumers, but often they produce an effect that is the opposite of the one intended.

Prior to the revision of the Bank Act in 1967, the banks were not supposed to charge more than 6 percent interest on personal loans. That sounds like a beneficial measure for consumers, but in practice it was of very little help. When the rate on National Housing Act mortgages went above 6 percent in 1959, some banks decided that it would be illegal to charge more than 6 percent so they stopped making NHA mortgage loans. Many consumers found that they could no longer get these loans from a bank. At the same time, some banks were charging 11 percent on personal loans because they had figured out another way of setting the charges to get the higher rate while still making it appear that the consumer was paying 6 percent.

The method for this piece of deception is a typical piece of statistical chicanery. You want to borrow $100. The banker says there is a $10 service charge, front-end load, or whatever the name he chooses. The end result is the same. You don't get $100, you get $90, but you pay interest on $100. In addition, you are paying off this loan over a year so you really have borrowed the $90 for 1 month and decreasing amounts each month after that. The interest you actually pay is therefore really a percentage of about $60, the amount you have on average over the year, not the $100 your interest rate is calculated on. The banks were not challenged on this inventive strategy and it effectively circumvented the ceiling on interest rates.

Nevertheless most banks did not push their personal lending or mortgage financing aggressively because of the ceiling on interest rates, and most consumers who wanted to borrow money for these purposes went to finance companies, often at higher rates. With removal of the 6 percent ceiling in 1967 the banks suddenly felt no hesitation in fighting for the business openly and aggressively, and the credit market changed radically.

In the succeeding thirteen years, the banks increased their personal loans by 9.7 times and their mortgages on residential property 22.1 times. The consumer benefited because more money was available for personal loans and mortgages and often at rates that were lower than other lenders charged. That is the reason why there was such a major shift in market shares in both consumer lending and mortgage financing in recent years.

One of the advantages of having economic power has always been the right to set prices. The OPEC cartel sets world oil prices, and for most of Canada's history, the bankers have set the price of banking services. They had a common schedule setting the rate they would all pay on savings deposits and the minimum rates they would all charge on most types of loans. The only areas which were subject to the competitive forces of the market place were personal instalment loans and loans made in foreign currencies.

The linchpin of this money cartel was the prime rate, the rate charged to the most favoured borrowers. Most other rates were set in series of steps from the prime rate, with savings accounts a good step down and loan rates at varying steps above. And just in case one hungry banker got aggressive ideas about taking customers away from another bank, the bankers also agreed that no bank would break this code by trying to lure a customer away from another bank by offering a lower interest rate or a larger line of credit. These uncompetitive practices were fully documented in 1964 in the Report of the Royal Commission on Banking and Finance.

The changes in the Bank Act and other factors which increased competition between financial institutions have led to somewhat less uniformity since that time. Nevertheless the main differences in rates still lie between types of financial institutions and not between financial institutions of the same kind. There is still a great similarity between rates charged by the five leading chartered banks for most bank-

ing services, as there is between the rates charged by the
leading trust companies. The differences arise more between the smaller, newer financial institutions and the
larger established ones because of the competitive battle
for a share of the market.

Another flaw in the competitive market for money that
sets interest rates is what is known as a cultural ceiling on
rates. Above a certain interest rate, the demand for money
at that price dries up rapidly even though there is an ample
supply. This appears to happen in the mortgage market
when interest rates approach 16 percent. At that price people become increasingly reluctant to take out mortgages to
buy houses.

The reasons for this situation are very complex, but one
significant factor is the impact of high rates on the monthly
payments. A twenty-five-year mortgage for $30,000 re-
quires monthly payments of $268.35 if the interest rate is
10 percent. At 12 percent, these payments would increase
to $309.57, and this may be more than the purchaser can
afford.

Consequently most prudent mortgage borrowers realize
that when interest rates reach a high level, they must borrow less to keep debt repayment to a prudent proportion of
their income. This hesitancy about increasing debt burden
may be reinforced if inflation is reducing purchasing
power. A family may have to spend more of its income on
food, children's clothing, or transportation.

Other families may have the opposite reaction. If
inflationary pressures are pushing up the price of housing,
but family income is rising, many people may increase
their borrowing at higher rates. They are gambling that the
house or other purchases will rise in value and compensate
them for the high cost of acquiring it.

Sensitivity of Consumers to Interest Rates

Academic studies done in the United States in the mid '70s after truth in lending legislation was introduced were pessimistic about its effectiveness because they concluded that consumers were not influenced in their purchase decisions by knowing the real interest rate on their borrowing. Fortunately, a later study done in 1977 indicated that this was no longer the case, that consumers were far more aware of the interest cost on their borrowings and that this influenced their credit decisions.

A 1970 study on this subject prepared in the United States for the National Commission on Consumer Finance found that:

> Despite the rise in consumer knowledge, the effect of disclosure on actual purchase behavior has been minimal. Some consumers reported that they might use the credit information in the future, but among those having used credit since TIL (Truth in Lending), knowledge about credit terms had very little influence on their comparison shopping, either among retailers or credit sources. In the decisions to postpone purchases or to use cash instead of credit, knowledge of credit terms played no role whatsoever.[2]

Eight years later, a new study reported that consumers had become much more aware of interest rates on their borrowings. The Survey Research Center of the University of Michigan was asked by the Federal Reserve Board, the Federal Deposit Insurance Corporation, and the Comptroller of the Currency (the three government agencies which control the federal banking system) to survey consumer awareness of credit costs. It found that in the ten years since lenders were forced to state their credit charges in clear language, the level of awareness of credit costs had risen sharply. The proportion of credit users who were aware of the annual percentage rates charged on bank credit cards had increased from 26.6 percent in 1969 to 71.3 percent in 1977. The lowest level of awareness occurred on loans for buying used cars, but even here there was a significant improvement from only 7.2 percent of consumers knowing the credit cost in 1969 to 38.3 percent in 1977. By contrast, knowledge of credit costs among buyers of new cars increased from 17.5 to 70.0 percent.[3]

The study also determined that consumers with higher incomes and more education were not only more aware, but they also showed the largest increase in awareness. However, all groups did show significant increases.

The results of this study show the importance of informing consumers fully and fairly about interest rates. As they become increasingly sensitive to interest rates, the rates will become more competitive and financial institutions will be prevented from overcharging or misleading consumers on the real cost of the money they borrow.

7

Per Astra Ad Ardua
—The Flaws in Deposit Insurance

A bank failure is a frightening thought to consumers. Those who lived through the Great Depression recall the anxiety and suffering caused by the 8,493 bank failures in the United States from 1929 to 1933 and the panic when all the banks closed their doors for three days in 1933.

Canadians liked to think that our banking institutions were too big, too strong, and too conservatively managed to get into financial trouble. That was basically correct. The chartered banks were all financially sound but that line of thinking completely overlooked the rest of the banking system, especially the smaller trust companies and credit unions. These financial institutions were just as capable of getting into hot water as any small American bank in the depression. In fact, a number of credit unions did get overextended and three trust companies failed. These financial disasters were a great shock to the depositors and

gave a black eye to the governments that were supposed to
be regulating them.

Fortunately most of the depositors were saved from a
major loss by the fact that their deposits were partially or
entirely insured by either a credit union insurance fund or
by the Canada Deposit Insurance Corporation. Today, all
banks and federally incorporated trust companies and
mortgage loan companies are required by law to pay a
fixed percentage of their deposits to the Canada Deposit
Insurance Corporation. In most cases, provincially incorporated companies, with the exception of Quebec-incor-
porated companies holding deposits in Quebec, are also
required to pay into the CDIC on a similar basis. The
Quebec companies support the Quebec Deposit Insurance
Board.

These levies create an insurance fund which can provide
consumers with a degree of financial compensation if their
banking institution fails. At the present time, the maximum
amount of the insurance is only $20,000, or one-half the
maximum in the United States. It should also be noted that
this maximum covers principal and interest combined. If
you have a $20,000 deposit that is supposed to pay 9 per-
cent interest, and the bank goes flat on its back, you get no
interest. Only your $20,000 is covered by insurance. This
insurance does, however, cover more than deposits. It includes all these financial services provided that they are
payable in Canada and in Canadian currency:

     —chequing accounts
     —savings accounts
     —money orders
     —deposit receipts
     —guaranteed investment certificates
     —debentures with a maximum term of five years

Some important additional features of deposit insurance are:

a.) the $20,000 maximum can cover a *package of all* eligible holdings in an insured institution. It is the combined total that matters.

b.) the $20,000 maximum covers deposits in *one* institution. You can spread your risk by depositing up to $20,000 in different institutions so that all your money is insured.

c.) contents of safety deposit boxes are not insured.

d.) joint accounts are insured separately.

e.) trust accounts are insured separately.

f.) payments on deposits in insolvent banks are usually settled within thirty days.

g.) RRSPs and RHOSPs are not insured but the contributions may be if they were placed in insured deposits like a savings account or a GIC. If the bank holding the deposits fails, the insurance will be paid to the trustee, not to the planholder.

Deposit insurance does not cost the consumer anything directly, nor do you have to apply for it. Your money is automatically insured when you deposit it. The banking institute is the one who pays directly through an annual premium of $\frac{1}{30}$ of 1 percent of all the insured deposits held by that institution.

The banks and trust companies think this method of assessing the insurance cost is very unfair to them because it takes no account of risk. A small or newly incorporated bank pays the same rate as a big established bank and a bank that puts its depositors' money into speculative investments pays the same rate as a bank that puts it all into Government of Canada Bonds. They claim that a fairer way to finance the CDIC would be to set rates that vary with the degree of risk. The trouble with variable rates is that they would be difficult to set and could be very expensive for a new bank.

The CDIC does not seem to have any intention of changing this rate. From time to time, there are also rumours of an increase in the maximum amount of the insurance but the secretary-treasurer of the CDIC, T. J. Davis, said in March 1979 that the directors had considered an increase but rejected it on the grounds that not enough accounts would be affected to warrant it.

How Adequate Is This Insurance Coverage?

The premium payments have built up a fund which so far has provided ample resources to meet its obligations. It has only had claims from the failure of three trust companies. The collapse of Commonwealth Trust Company in Vancouver cost it $7 million. The failure of Security Trust Company led to claims of $10 million but in this case the CDIC was fully reimbursed by the Alberta government.

A widespread collapse of the banking system would be a different story, but it is important to remember that its own resources are not the limit of the CDIC's financial resources. The CDIC can also borrow from the Consolidated Revenue Fund of Canada and that provides sufficient cushion for almost any eventuality.

Nevertheless, if any consumer thinks that deposit insurance provides all the protection anyone needs, take a close look at what happened when Astra Trust Company closed its doors in the spring of 1980. Then take a close look at where you are putting your money before it is too late.

Astra Trust Company was formed in 1977 by a forty-six-year-old Quebecer named Carlo Montemurro, a supersalesman who learned how to promote securities in the late 1960s from one of the greatest rogues in the business, Bernie Cornfeld of IOS fame. Would you buy a used car from this man? Probably not, but many people were quite willing to hand over their personal savings to him.

Montemurro was able to create a small financial empire around Astra through interlocking directorates and common share ownership. Two other companies, C & M Financial Consultants and ReMor Investment Management Corporation, were used to manage mortgage investments and sell savings certificates to the public while Astra flogged the usual trust company services such as chequing and savings accounts, guaranteed investment certificates, and RRSPs. Before the Canada Deposit Insurance Corporation moved in, Astra had expanded from its head office in Niagara Falls to branch offices in Kitchener, St. Catharines, Burlington, Welland, and Hamilton. It had 1,750 customers holding deposits in chequing and savings accounts adding up to $4 million, as well as 2,600 customers holding $13.9 million in guaranteed investment certificates.

These customers had been lulled into a false sense of security by a misunderstanding of deposit insurance or perhaps by that fallacious term "trust company." The Canada Deposit Insurance Corporation belatedly took over control of Astra on April 24, 1980, too late for its shareholders, for many of its depositors, or for some investors in associated companies. This can of worms will provide at least three years entertainment for the police fraud squad, bankruptcy trustees, and related lawyers and accountants.

In defiance of law or sound business practice, Astra was facing a $367,000 loss on two consumer loans; it had loaned $122,000 to Montemurro and $420,000 to Canadian Recycling Laboratories, a company affiliated with former employees, without sufficient collateral; it had made loans on all of its furniture and fixtures to C & M Financial; it had a loss of $877,000 when its directors defaulted on their payments to a disastrous $2 million condominium project in Estepona, Spain; only 38 percent of its $18 million mortgage portfolio was insured; and there were numerous financial problems associated with land holdings and other unsound loans and mortgages.

Astra is now being wound up, ReMor is in bankruptcy, and C & M Financial is bankrupt and its three top officers are now facing criminal charges of fraud and theft. For its shareholders, the future is bleak, obviously. Astra has a total deficit of about $3.6 million if substantial provision is made for anticipated losses. That wipes out the shareholders' equity and leaves a final deficit of $1.2 million. There is also a $7 million claim against Astra laid by the trustee in bankruptcy for ReMor Investments who charges that the money invested by the public in this mortgage company was diverted improperly into Astra.

For the people who have their savings tied up in the Astra group of companies, the outcome varies from bleak to satisfactory. Everyone is a loser to some degree but some stand to lose more than others. The shareholders of Astra will get nothing. Investors in affiliated companies face significant losses. Holders of Registered Retirement Savings Plans invested in a mortgage fund administered separately by Astra may receive most of their $1.5 million, if another trust company will take over the administration of the fund. All the American students who placed their savings in American dollar accounts have found out to their regret that deposits of foreign currency are not insured, and they face substantial losses. Anyone who was owed more than $20,000 in principal and interest in insurable accounts or certificates will likely see little of this money.

Some lucky people will emerge from this enlightening experience with only a few bruises. Claims were met up to the $20,000 maximum for RRSPs, agency investment certificates, chequing and savings accounts, term deposits, and GICs. However, there was a period of many weeks during which most of these funds were locked up in the trust company. Only $2,000 could be withdrawn, a concession made by Canada Deposit Insurance Corporation to prevent too much hardship for Astra's customers. This meant that the public had no use of their accounts from June 13, when the assets of Astra were frozen by a court order, until at least July 31, when payment on insured accounts and money due before August 1 was paid. GICs and term deposits maturing after August 1 were paid a month later.

The big question that remains is, Why did it happen? Why would so many people have placed their faith and their money in a small trust company that had only been in business for three years? And why did the CDIC not spot the trouble earlier? John Cunningham, a St. Catharines lawyer representing a group of ReMor depositors, feels so strongly about the government's role that he is planning to charge it with failing to exercise sufficient care in supervising Astra. The Federal Superintendent of Insurance, Richard Humphreys, is quoted in *Maclean's* as saying that "we moved in on Astra as soon as we became aware of what was going on, but we still couldn't be there every day. This one got away on us and it doesn't make us very happy."[1]

This sounds depressingly familiar to any student of Canadian financial history. Back in 1969, Commonwealth Trust of Vancouver collapsed from similar causes, leaving a trail of fraud, misrepresentation, misallocation of funds, and tangled intercorporate dealings, which showed that the federal authorities still had not filled in the gaps in public protection revealed by the earlier default of British Mortgage and Trust, which had led directly to the founding of CDIC.

Many of the factors which led to the downfall of Commonwealth Trust had been fully documented over a year earlier in a thesis prepared at Simon Fraser University on the regulation of trust companies in British Columbia.[2] There, as well as in the Astra case, one of the key causes was the problem of provincial versus federal jurisdiction. In Commonwealth's case, the provincial authorities did not supervise the company and its affiliates as they should have. Why? is the question. Because the trust company was under federal jurisdiction while the associated companies were under provincial jurisdiction.

To really understand the complexities of deposit insurance and the problems that can arise, it is helpful to look back at the start of the Canada Deposit Insurance Corporation and the last years of British Mortgage and Trust.

British Mortgage and Trust

The leading financial institution for seventy-seven years in the small Ontario city of Stratford was British Mortgage and Trust. It was the only trust company there and it held the savings deposits of more people than all the banks rolled into one. Local organizations used its community room; it gave a $1,600 scholarship each year to a student entering university; it put $5.00 into a bank account for each grade twelve student making honours; and it was on all the lists for prize donors at country fairs. Many residents even owned shares in the company that they had inherited from their grandparents.

But appearances were deceiving. The more astute residents of Stratford noted in the early 1960s that the company was changing in many ways. They saw that after Wilfred P. Gregory, Q.C., became managing director in 1957 and then president in 1963, it increasingly became a one-man show with a reputation for investing money in places that trust companies ordinarily shunned. But since earnings were rising rapidly and so was the stock, most people wondered what there was to worry about. After all, Gregory should have known what he was doing. He had been a bencher of the Upper Canada Law Society and chairman of the Ontario section of the Trust Companies Association. He had held ten directorships and was a member of the Canada Council, and there was no reason not to believe him when he reported on June 7, 1965, that assets had increased by $9 million to a total of $120 million and predicted even greater growth in the future.

Few people were prepared when, within a week, the foundations of this house of cards began to shake. A large finance company, Atlantic Acceptance, went bankrupt and the rumour mills started turning. The shares of BMT were down from a high of $44 to $30, and then they suddenly dropped to $8.00. Only the directors knew why until it finally came out that BMT had loaned $8,700,000 to Atlantic, including a $640,000 personal loan to Powell Morgan, Atlantic's president. If that was not bad enough, it also was revealed that BMT had $10,185,000 on the books in bad mortgages. These combined losses were enough to wipe out the entire shareholders' equity.

A caretaker president, Harold Lawson, tried desperately to salvage something for the shareholders and stave off a run on the deposit accounts. But one of the biggest banks and the Trust Companies Association said, "No way."

In a speech to the Canadian Club in November 1965, Lawson told how shocked he was by this attitude.

> I do not like to say things like this and I am not saying that the bank was wrong. There is a moral dilemma. Should a bank or any other corporation put its own interests and the interests of its own shareholders above the interests of the community at large?
>
> It is hard to say. There are arguments in favour of what the bank did but these arguments do not appeal to me.
>
> I only know there were millions of dollars for investment companies to loan to people who want to "borrow confidently from folks they trust" but there was not one red cent for all those thousands of little people across the province who had saved their money and put their trust in British Mortgage.

Finally Victoria and Grey Trust offered to amalgamate on the basis of one share of V & G for six shares of BMT. That put a price of only $2.65 on BMT's shares, but the shareholders had no choice but to accept. As the rumours about BMT spread through the community, anxious depositors lined up at the teller's wicket to withdraw their money. By mid September, 68 percent of the deposits had been withdrawn and the only reason for most of the remaining 32 percent still being there was that the directors had not revealed the extent of the financial mess. If they had, BMT would have been cleaned out.

That would have been serious enough but the bankruptcy would have had much wider repercussions. The collapse of one trust company could easily have produced a ripple effect leading to runs on perfectly sound companies. Banks collapsed like dominoes during the depression of the 1930s in the United States in just that way.

The American response to the widening bank crisis of that time was to form the Federal Deposit Insurance Corporation to provide some level of insurance for all depositors in insured bank institutions. At the present time, all deposits are insured to a maximum of $40,000.

It is important to realize though that the major purpose of deposit insurance is not to protect depositors. Its real purpose is to reduce or prevent runs on the bank which can lead to insolvency of one bank and then spread through the banking system to other banks. The FDIC tries to prevent this by supervision and inspection of bank assets, but if the worst happens and a bank becomes insolvent, the FDIC tries to arrange a merger with a solvent bank. In this case, the depositors are not reimbursed by the insurance fund. Their deposits are just transferred to the merged company. In this way, all depositors are protected against loss, including those with deposits that are above the $40,000 insurance limit.

That is the way it worked at BMT too. The depositors and the holders of guaranteed investment certificates were salvaged by the merger with V & G. But if that had not happened they could have lost all their money. The holders of GICs were in a particularly weak position because they could not pull their money out before the GIC matured.

The Canadian government had stuck its head in the sand for too long on the subject of bank failures. It assumed that the American experience was from a different world. Canada had not had a bank failure since the Home Bank collapsed in 1923, while the United States had had 183 from 1946 to 1977. Part of the reason for all these bank failures was the very large number of small banks in the United States, but Canadian authorities were overlooking the fact that Canadians were turning in greater and greater numbers to new banking institutions to get better interest rates and cheaper banking services.

The BMT fiasco finally awakened the Canadian government to the fact that failure could happen here, and we had no deposit insurance to protect the investor. The result was the birth of the Canada Deposit Insurance Corporation in 1967. This organization is designed, like its U.S. counterpart, to protect the banking system from loss of public confidence.

What has been the impact of the CDIC? There is no doubt that it has improved the quality of the insured banking institutions. The banks were already inspected by the Inspector General of Banks but now all insured trust companies and mortgage loan companies are inspected by the Federal Superintendent of Insurance. There is some question about the quality of the mortgage lending by a few of the smaller companies, but in general the consumer can feel a lot safer.

The other noticeable beneficiary of deposit insurance is the small or new banking institution. Consumers feel far more comfortable about leaving their money in these companies if they are covered by insurance. Many people spread their savings among several of these smaller banks to get their higher interest rates. In that way deposit insurance has encouraged competition by making it easier for new companies to get started, and consumers benefit from the increased competition by getting a greater variety of savings instruments at a better price.

You may have noticed that credit unions are not covered by the CDIC. They have their own method of "insuring" deposits, although it varies from province to province. In British Columbia, for example, deposits are protected by the Provincial Credit Union Share and Deposit Guarantee Fund which is managed by the Credit Union Reserve Board. All deposits as well as interest and dividends on credit union shares are guaranteed, so it is practically correct to say that these deposits are 100 percent insured.

Other areas in Canada have different methods of guaranteeing deposits but they are based usually on a provincial fund, and if necessary, the national organization, Canadian Co-operative Credit Society. The provincial or territorial government may even assist if necessary. Four credit unions in the Northwest Territories got into serious problems in 1978 when they accumulated losses of $900,000. Adverse economic conditions in this area were a factor to some degree, but poor management certainly played a big part.

They had a large number of unsecured or poorly secured loans which were not collectable and had made loans at rates which were too low to cover the cost of administering them. The government of the N.W.T. suspended the board of directors and announced that it would guarantee all credit union deposits in the N.W.T. About $750,000 of the loss was covered by the Mutual Aid Depository Fund. The Canadian Co-operative Credit Society paid $50,000 and the N.W.T. government covered the remaining $100,000 loss.

Similar rescue operations have taken place in other parts of Canada. Credit unions are now getting far more scrutiny and enforced accountability from their central organization. If a credit union appears to be in a financially shaky position, the central will move in examiners and management staff and clean up the situation. Then it will closely monitor the credit union to be sure that it does not lapse. That would seem to indicate that any credit union belonging to a central organization provides adequate protection for its members.

Consumers must realize though that a bank, a trust company, or a credit union can still lose money for its depositors, investors, and shareholders. No regulatory authority can possibly watch over all the day-to-day transfers of money, and unfortunately their very frequency and complexity make it possible for an adroit manipulator of money to pull off a financial coup. The CDIC could check every dime one month and a month later the till could be cleaned right out. It is just in the nature of the business that it creates great opportunities for fraud, and consequently it presents great temptation and attracts people with that in mind.

It is important to realize also that some consumers must share the blame when financial institutions default. They are so greedy for an extra 1 percent interest that they will place their precious savings with companies that would never stand up to close scrutiny.

Before putting money on deposit, find out how large the company is, how long it has been in business, and what kind of services it provides. Make sure that you are dealing directly with the company and not with a subsidiary that operates outside the regulation of the CDIC. Do not rely on an employee of the company to tell you if your deposit or investment is insured, because far too many employees of these companies do not know much about deposit insurance.

PART TWO

The Consumer

The Consumer

8

Chequing Accounts

Canadians wrote between four and nine million cheques on their accounts in chartered banks on every business day in 1980. That added up to about 2.0 billion cheques for the year, double the number written ten years before. And these figures do not include all the "cheques" written on accounts at trust companies and credit unions.

The daily value of the cheques written on bank accounts averages from $12 billion to $16 billion. On an annual basis that amounts to close to $5.3 trillion—about 23 times the entire production of goods and services in Canada. Ten years ago, the value of cheques cashed in banks was only about $796 million daily. The amount of money held in chequing accounts has not increased nearly as quickly, which means that Canadians are turning over the money in their chequing accounts much faster. This turnover has, in fact, increased very rapidly. Ten years ago, the cheques written by Canadians in a day were equal to about 1/5 of their average chequing deposits. Today this has been increased to 3 times average deposits.

Only Americans write more cheques in a year than Canadians; 50 percent more than Canadians on a per capita basis. Other countries write far fewer cheques per person and settle much higher percentages of their financial transactions by cash. Great Britain, for example, pays only 60 percent of its bills by cheque, while Canadians pay 90 percent in that manner.

The chequing system is obviously vitally important to Canadians and it must be operated with efficiency and equity. To this end, the banks have spent huge sums on automation in order to reduce the work and time involved in processing those 4 million pieces of paper a day through the system. We now have such developments as on-line banking, providing the teller with direct information about your account, automatic tellers, and multiple branch banking. Unfortunately we also have computer breakdowns, errors, fraud, and theft. There are few legal safeguards for the customer who relies on paperless bookkeeping.

The Consumers' Association in British Columbia conducted a survey to find out what kind of problems people had with their bank transactions. Thirty-two percent reported incorrect amounts credited, 6 percent reported that deposits had not been credited in time, 19 percent had incorrect debits, 12 percent had incorrect pay-roll deductions, 12 percent had been refused payment on a cheque or draft, and 19 percent had a variety of other errors. These problems are not always due to the use of computers; in many cases, they are just a result of the greater size and complexity of the banking system.

On the other hand, new developments in the chequing system provide benefits for the consumer who takes the time to comparison-shop for the best chequing service and who avoids the pitfalls found in some banking services. The principal areas that must be watched are chequing charges, package accounts, interest payments, hidden costs, and un-disclosed bank policies or ones that are not adequately disclosed.

Do You Know That:

A cheque is legally a cheque only if it is drawn on an ac-count at a bank.

A so-called "cheque" written on an account at a trust company or a credit union is not legally a cheque. It is only a payment order. "The result," according to the Law Reform Commission of Canada "is to create a series of legal traps for the users of such instruments."[1]

The root of the problem here is that a cheque is gov-erned by an anachronistic piece of legislation called the Bills of Exchange Act which has had no searching review since its inception shortly after Confederation. In a modern monetary economy, "cheques" on trust companies and credit unions as well as on banks vie with all sorts of com-puter-based payments and the law on money should be up-dated to recognize this new world.

Do You Know What Those Funny Numbers at the Bottom of Your Cheques Mean?

All cheques issued by Canadian banks have three sets of characters in a special computer-oriented typeface printed in magnetic ink on a 5/16-inch-deep band across the centre bottom edge of the cheque. This is MICR—mag-netic ink character recognition—and it was one of the early devices used in the automation of business systems.

The first set of numbers on a cheque gives the location

and name of the branch on which the cheque is drawn. The second set gives the name of the bank involved. The third set gives the account number of the person writing the cheque.

These cheques can be sorted automatically at high speeds by machines which read MICR. But sometimes the bank wishes these machines could read more than MICR. In an article on computer crime in the October 1980 issue of *B.C. Business,* the story was told of a bank customer who replaced the blank deposit slips at the counters in his bank with deposit slips that had his account number code printed on the bottom. For four wonderful days, the bank's computer credited all these deposits to his account— $100,000 worth.

Who Pays When Your Cheque Is Altered?

Suppose you write "3" on a cheque, leaving a blank space after the figure on the written amount. Then somebody fills in those spaces with a thousand and cashes the cheque on your account for $3,000. Who pays?

You do, because you were negligent in drawing the cheque and this negligence made it easy for someone else to alter the cheque. To write a cheque properly, start the amount of the cheque in words at the extreme left of the space provided and line out unused space to the right.

What Are the Different Types of Chequing Accounts?

The simplest form of chequing account is a personal chequing account which pays no interest and charges the customer a flat fee for every cheque written. The major chartered banks all have these accounts and most charge $.18 for every cheque that is written on that account.

It is possible to avoid this charge at a few banking institutions. This service sounds good at first glance but processing a cheque costs the bank $.50 to $.75, so somebody is paying for it. Free chequing is really a "loss leader" to get savings accounts and general banking business.

There are variations of the standard chequing account: (1) accounts that pay a low rate of interest, (2) that require a minimum balance in the account, and (3) that are part of a package of banking services. These variations need to be closely examined because they are not all they seem on the surface.

Watch Out for These Traps

1. *Savings-chequing accounts*—This is the least advantageous type of chequing account, yet many people prefer it. These accounts usually pay 3 percent interest per year on the minimum balance during a six-month period and then magnanimously allow one free cheque a month for every $100 in the account. After that you pay $.20 a cheque.

Banks claim that they tried to eliminate these accounts, but customers wanted them because they provide convenient one-account banking in place of having both a chequing and a savings account. But that means it is neither flesh nor fowl and this is clearly a controversial subject. On the consumer's side, columnist Lorne Parton wrote in the Vancouver *Express* that "both the Commerce and the Royal are pushing another 'service' in ad campaigns. The service is for the savings-chequing account, and the ads are pushed at that segment of the young population about to set out on its own." After comparing the features, Parton goes on to say:

> Curiously, when asked about it, both banks replied in almost identical terms: They tried to phase out the savings-chequing account, but so many people liked the convenience of one-account banking that they were forced to re-think the situation and thus decided to cash-in (my words) on the demand. You might call it McDonald's style banking: Quick, simple and convenient, and that's what you pay for.
>
> The Royal added that its people have been trained to "cross-sell" to tell the customer brought in by the chequing-savings ads about the advantages of the other services. A kind of reverse-English bait-and-switch, you might say.[2]

Others are incensed about elderly people holding large sums of money in these accounts for years and writing only a few cheques each year. One concerned consumer wrote me to say, "Several years ago, I discovered my own elderly father was allowed to keep $20,000 in a chequing account at 3 percent when his bank was offering 8½ percent on its true savings accounts. At that time he wrote about three cheques a year and was obviously losing a lot of money."

Senior bank personnel have a somewhat different story. A manager at the Bank of Montreal commented that elderly people used this type of account to hold down their interest income because they would have to pay tax on any amount over $1,000! Another bank manager added that customers used this type of account because they believed they actually were ahead financially. A pity they were not advised how very wrong they were.

For most people, the best combination is a personal chequing account and a savings account that pays interest on the daily balance.

Western Canadians have a better option at the Bank of B.C. The Bonanza Account requires a minimum balance of $500, but, if you can provide that, it pays interest every month on the daily balance. You receive a monthly statement with your cancelled cheques and pay $.25 for each cheque or withdrawal. For the person who writes only a few cheques a month, this type of account is the answer.

2. *Minimum Balance Accounts*—Many banks have a type of account which allows "free" chequing provided the customer always has a set minimum balance in the account. Of course the cheques are not free at all because that money could be earning interest in a savings account. An amount of $500 left in an account for a year at 9.5 percent interest could earn $47.50. That sum would pay for 263 cheques a year or 22 a month. Most people do not write that many cheques in a month so the minimum balance account really overcharges them for their "free" chequing.

Customers using minimum balance accounts incur an additional loss if they deposit a large sum like a pay cheque and draw it down progressively over two weeks or a month. In this case, the average daily balance over the month will be much higher than the required minimum monthly balance and the bank is getting the use of this additional money at no cost to itself.

From the customer's point of view, the best system is one which would use a minimum balance that was an average of the daily balances in the account. A large amount could then be deposited once or twice a month and then cheques could be written on the account to bring it down below the minimum by the end of the month.

In practice then, this type of account should only be used by customers who write a considerable number of cheques. If the number of cheques written each year times

$.18 is greater than the forgone interest on the minimum monthly balance, it is most probably a good deal.

3. *Package Accounts*—The attractive blue brochure has the typical picture of the attentive well-dressed young couple and the smiling employee. The incongruous thing that catches the eye is the background, showing shelves of china (collector's items?) enclosed behind leaded panes of glass. When was the last time you saw that in a deposit institution?

Perhaps this is what alerts the skeptical consumer that something strange is going on here. The front page reads "Guaranty Service—All the Financial Services you're likely to need for only $2.50 a month." Inside it goes on to say "Guaranty Service eliminates separate charges on most day-to-day financial services and provides you with special cost reductions on other more personalized Guaranty Trust products."

Further on, it says you will receive a personalized Guaranty Service Card (just what most consumers have always wanted), unlimited free chequing, personalized cheques and a cheque wallet free of charge, free transfers between accounts, no commissions on travellers cheques or money orders, and free direct deposit of cheques.

That raises the question of why you are paying $2.50 a month, $30.00 a year, since all these items are free. You do get $5.00 off your safety deposit box charge each year and ¼ percent off your interest on a personal loan. But maybe you do not want a personal loan or a safety deposit box. The only thing you are paying for in that case is the personalized Guaranty Service Card. This will apparently identify you at any branch of the Guaranty Trust as a special customer entitled to all the benefits and courtesy of

Guaranty Service. It seems like a lot to pay for politeness from a teller.

The Bank of British Columbia was the first Canadian bank to use a package, which it introduced as a "Western Account." The larger banks soon followed suit and then some of the trust companies decided to jump on the bandwagon. The economics of this type of account leave a great deal to be desired for many customers. Older people in particular have been encouraged to sign up for these packages even though they have little need or use for them. On a general level it is a backward move at a time when computerization of banking services should lead to much more efficient cost accounting for different banking services. It is much easier now to charge the user of banking services for a particular function, because the banks know what it costs to provide each service. Under these circumstances, all accounts should pay a fair rate of interest on the daily balance and make a specific charge for each service used by the customer. Then the banking system would be allocating banking resources more efficiently because consumers would be less likely to overuse facilities by writing cheques excessively.

Customers can also be misled easily by the package deals into thinking that they will save money. The Royal Bank points that out in their brochure for Royal Certified Services, a package deal that costs $4.00 a month. The bank says that "Frankly, not everyone can enjoy equal benefit from Royal Certified Service. But if you frequently pay bills by cheque, would like a Safety Deposit Box, would appreciate a preferential rate on Termplan Personal Loans, or if you could benefit from the other useful facilities in the package, then this offer may be right for you."

Anyone thinking of paying for a package account should

look at it carefully. Take all the costs and all the benefits
item by item to find out if you would really save money.

Using the Royal as an example, a typical analysis would
look like this:

Benefit	Cost	Cost/Benefit
Personalized service card to use at any Royal Bank branch	None	Very little benefit to the average consumer but of great benefit to the bank because it assigns a customer a Personal Identification Number
Unlimited chequing	$4 a month	Equal to 17 cheques at 18¢ a cheque. Most people do not write this many cheques in a month
Overdraft protection for a short period of time and a maximum of $300	No charge on overdrawn cheque but interest charged on amount overdrawn on monthly basis	Could be very expensive if large sum is overdrawn for a few days because interest will be charged for a full month
Cheque cashing coast to coast	None	Useful to a few people. Available free with Master-Card card at Bank of Montreal
Personalized cheques with name, address, and telephone number	None	$3.25 charge to other customers. May be easier to cash, but not necessary
No commission on travellers cheques	None	Normally pay 1% commission at bank but available free at some financial institutions
No charge on money orders	None	$.25
Bill payments	None	Banks usually charge $.25 per per bill but service is available free at some banking institutions
Safe deposit box or safekeeping	Annual reduction of $9.50 or 79¢ a month	Covers cost of small box or safekeeping for a few securities
Automatic transfers to savings accounts	None	Would be a lot more help if it worked the other way— automatic transfers from savings to chequing account

Reduction on personal loans	None	Benefits only those who borrow at this bank
Visa card	None	Customers must take out a Visa card even if they do not want it. No charge for card if you don't have a package account so no benefit. Benefit to bank because it gets customer using it
		Loss of privacy through credit and background check

From this analysis, it is obvious that a high-powered bank customer who travels and spends freely would likely be ahead with a package account. The customer who writes ten cheques a month, seldom travels or borrows money, and manages his financial affairs circumspectly loses with a package account. The calculation is different for everyone.

Consumer Reports, published in January 1975, has been particularly critical of these plans. In their view, a package account

> . . . can be, in fact, one of the most expensive and unnecessary accounts a consumer can choose.
>
> Bankers concede that such package accounts benefit only the minority of customers who make very heavy use of every type of bank service. But many of the services offered in package accounts are used by a small fraction of those paying for such accounts; safe deposit boxes and personal loan discounts are used by far less than 50 per cent of package customers. Moreover, a number of the services advertized as part of the package—for example bank credit cards and overdraft privileges (prearranged lines of credit that allow you to write cheques for more than you actually have on deposit in your chequing account) are commonly available without charge to *all* depositors, whether or not they have a package account.[3]

This is only one of the ways in which much of the advertising for package accounts is very misleading. Some of the ads tell customers that they get "free" chequing, "free" transfers between accounts, "free" travellers cheques, but these same customers are paying $30 to $48 a year for these "free" services. Clearly they are paying, and paying plenty in some cases.

There are other examples of misleading advertising. The ads for the Key Account of the Canadian Imperial Bank of Commerce talk about free overdraft protection, but it is hardly free. In fact it can be very expensive.

The customary charge to a customer who overdraws his account is $2.00. With a Key Account, the customer does not get billed $2.00. Instead, the customer gets billed much more, because the amount of the account that is overdrawn automatically becomes an advance on the customer's Visa account and is immediately charged interest at a rate of 21 percent. That is bad enough, but what is even worse is that there is a minimum amount of $50 on which the interest is charged, and furthermore interest is charged on a monthly basis. Overdraw your account by $10 for three days and you pay 21 percent for a month on $50. This is a feature of the Key Account that is not spelled out in any of the advertising.

The Bank of Montreal is somewhat more explicit. In talking about Overdraft Protection on a Firstbank Full Service Package, they say:

> Avoid the embarrassment and inconvenience of N.S.F. cheques. You have a choice—either a temporary "payday" overdraft up to a $300 limit on your checking account—or a cash advance on your Master Charge account in multiples of $50. Interest on a Master Charge cash advance is charged at a rate of 1¾% a month (21% per annum) from the date of the advance until payment is received at the Master Charge payment centre. Interest at the same rate is charged on chequing account overdrafts subject to a $2.00 minimum.

One of the most objectionable aspects of all package accounts at the five largest banks is the requirement that the customer must apply for and qualify for a bank credit card. At the Royal, the Commerce, the TD (Toronto-Dominion), and the Nova Scotia, the customers must get a Visa card and at the Montreal they must get a MasterCard card. You cannot have a package account without one.

This is the most insidious aspect of the package account. It means, for one thing, that you must allow the bank to make a thorough credit check on you even though there may be no valid reason to do so. A customer who buys most of these services separately does not have to agree to a credit check. Nor do they have to qualify for a credit card. A credit check is needed only for personal loans and overdraft privileges. The only advantage of this compulsory credit check to the customer is that loans can be obtained much faster. You do not have to wait for credit approval if you want to borrow money.

From the bank's point of view, it makes a great deal of sense to get the spenders (and usually borrowers) in our society onto credit cards as soon as possible. It sets them on the path to the cashless society. The personal identification card also helps in this way because it assigns each customer a personal identification number and this PIN will be an integral part of the electronic funds transfer system (EFTS). In the meantime, the credit cards are extremely profitable to the banks because they encourage people to spend more and to borrow more, and on credit cards they borrow at rates that are higher than they would pay on a mortgage or a personal loan.

Forcing a customer to get a credit rating and a credit card also adds greatly to the bank's data base on each customer. A frequent user of credit cards provides the bank with a mass of information on consumer buying patterns, incomes, saving tendencies, and use of banking services, all of which can be retrieved and analyzed to produce new

CHARACTERISTICS OF CHARTERED BANKS

	Bank of British Columbia	The Royal Bank of Canada	Canadian Imperial Bank of Commerce
Name of Account	Western	Certified Service	Key Account
Monthly Charge	$4.00	$4.00	$4.00
Eligibility	19 years of age and over	must qualify for Visa Account	must qualify for Visa Account
Chequing Account Features include:			
Indentification Card	yes	yes	yes
Personalized cheques	yes	yes	yes
Unlimited chequing	yes	yes	yes
Transfer to Savings Accounts	yes	yes	yes
Required Minimum Balance	none	none	none
Interest Paid	4% on minimum quarterly balance over $100	none	none
Deposit Facilities			free use of 24-hr. depository
Payment of Utility Bills	no charge	no charge	no charge
Free Money Orders	domestic	any currency	domestic
Travellers Cheques	no charge	no charge	no charge
Cheque Cashing	no charge any branch	no charge any branch up to $500	no charge any branch up to $500
Overdraft Protection	cheques covered up to prearranged $1,500 limit	up to $500	advance up to Visa limit
Safety Deposit Box	standard box included	allowance of $12 a year	preferred rates
Safekeeping		allowance of $12 a year	
Other Features	free wallet		no charge for use of 24-hr. cash

"Package Accounts" (January 1981)

Toronto-Dominion Bank	The Bank of Nova Scotia	Bank of Montreal	Regular Individual Charges
Personal Service Plan	Scotia Club	Full Service Package	
$4.00	$3.25	$4.00	
must qualify for Visa Account	must qualify for Visa Account	must qualify for MasterCard Account	
no	yes	yes	$3.25
yes	yes	yes	$.16–$.18 per cheque
yes	yes	yes	
yes	yes	yes	
none	none	none	
none	none	none	
any branch free, "letter-slot" deposits	any branch free, and night depository		
no charge	no charge	no charge	
any currency	any currency	any currency	$.35–.55 on $100 or less; $.35 on $151–$500
no charge	no charge	no charge	1% commission
no charge any branch up to $500	no charge any branch up to approved credit	no charge any branch	$.20–.25 per cheque
automatic advance up to Visa limit	automatic advance up to Visa limit	automatic advance up to MasterCard limit or $300 overdraft	
allowance of $2.50 a year	not offered	allowance of $10	$12–18
		allowance of $9.50 a year	
same charges and privileges for joint accounts	free wallet; monthly fee guaranteed for 12 mos. from approval of application	mail-in deposit; 24-hour deposit	

gimmicks to lure the customer into using more banking services. This is known as cross-selling and it will become a bigger and bigger marketing technique to manipulate customers in the years ahead.

Some banks offer a better deal to consumers who are sixty to sixty-five years of age or older. The Bank of B.C. has a Pioneer Service Plan that offers similar benefits to the Royal Certified Plan but at no charge for it. It also makes an annual adjustment to the monthly interest on savings accounts for inflation.

The Personalized Cheques Con

The Toronto *Globe and Mail* carried an interesting story a couple of years ago headed up "Just Who Can You Trust?"

> Sometimes it's best to resist a sales pitch, or so some customers of Guaranty Trust are finding out.
>
> The company is telling customers they must buy new personalized cheques. However, it will provide free cheques if the sales pitch fails.
>
> "If you convince your customers to purchase cheques, you'll save for your (company) branch too because your branch is charged for the ones we give away to customers," says a recent internal document called Mostly Marketing.
>
> A good sales pitch is to tell the customer that Guaranty Trust will "soon be requiring our customers to have personalized cheques for clearing purposes." This catches the customer's attention and creates an interest "by telling her why she has to buy. You've also indicated a sense of action and urgency by asking for the order today," the memo says.
>
> Every customer will have to have personalized cheques soon, but "if Mrs. Jones still doesn't go for it, then offer the free cheques. Better for the branch to pay than lose a customer."
>
> Company marketing executives said the document was in-

tended only for the staff. "Why should The Globe and Mail offer the paper free to some people while the next person down the hall is paying? It's the same thing," Diane McPherson, manager of marketing services, said.

Miss McPherson said the memo should have told employees to explain to customers why they "should buy and not why they have to buy. We're learning."

For a book of 200 cheques, customers pay $3.85, according to the marketing manager—or $4.10, according to a branch manager. These cheques have the customer's name and account number printed on a scenic background. The customer who doesn't want to buy them gets a free book of personalized cheques without the scenic background.

Miss McPherson said Guaranty Trust wanted to give customers the option of buying fancy cheques. She would not say how much the free cheques cost the company.

The sales program is successful so far, according to the memo, but "we'd like to offer some final day reminders to help you boost sales and qualify for one of those nifty prizes."

The memo was sent to employees in 47 branches across Canada. The company wants to change over to a system requiring personalized cheques by the end of the year.[4]

Gold Cheques from the Commerce

In the spring of 1975, the Commerce announced that it was introducing Gold cheques and Lorne Parton in his consumer column in the Vancouver *Express* wondered how the convenience that costs could ever have been dreamed up:

I imagine it happened this way:

The top hot-shots of the Commerce Bank are huddled in a storm session at head office. Off in a corner, Anne Murray is crooning the corporate theme song. In the middle of the shiny mahogany table sits a Visa card, and besides it visual aids labeled "Eaton's," "Simpsons," "Sears," and so forth.

"This is the problem, gentlemen," says No. 1 Hot-shot.

"How to get this . . ." he picks up the Visa Card ". . . into these . . ." and he slips the card under one of the Eaton's aids.

"As you know, the Bay is the only large chain that takes our Visa. The others have kept it out so they can get the credit action with their in-house cards. What can we do about it?"

There is a furious silence broken only by Anne Murray's humming. Finally, Cretchley, the junior brainstormer, clears his throat. "This might be right off the wall, chief, but I'll let it fly and see if anybody shoots at it. The stores accept personal cheques, right?"

"Right."

"So, we set up a system where people can write cheques, not in their chequing accounts, but on their Visa accounts!"

By this time he has their complete attention, and even Anne stops crooning to listen.

"Here's the nice part," continues the encouraged Cretchley. "As soon as those cheques are charged to the customer's account, they start incurring interest, same as a cash withdrawal!"

There is a pregnant silence and the head honcho rises to his feet, clears his straw hat from his head and Frisbees it out the window. "Mr. Cretchley," he booms, "I take my hat off to you!"

And so it comes to pass. The Commerce has now introduced "Gold Cheques . . . a new service from Commerce Chargex."[5]

The introductory brochure makes for fascinating reading to a student of banking hype. It invites us all to jump on the bandwagon and spend, spend, spend.

Now you can take advantage of that great sale item in your favorite department store, or, from the comfort of your own home, conveniently meet those unexpected emergencies, automobile or home repairs, property or income taxes, or insurance premiums.

You can use your new Commerce Chargex Gold Cheques.

As a new feature of your Chargex account, we will provide you with special personalized Gold Cheques which can be used to pay for goods or services where your card is not yet accepted but you can pay by cheque.

Gold Cheques are regular personalized cheques, but they're payable out of your Chargex account. Any payments you make using your Gold Cheques will be identified on your monthly Chargex statement as "Gold Cheque" and treated as cash advance transactions so that Gold Cheques will be subject to the regular Chargex rate (1½ % per month, 18% per annum) from the date these cheques are charged to your account. So it is still in your best interest to continue to use your Chargex card wherever possible for regular purchases.

Take advantage now of the added convenience and versatility Commerce Chargex Gold Cheques will offer you. Remember, you can write Gold Cheques up to the unused portion of your available credit limit.

Simply fill out the attached form, enclose it with your regular Chargex payment or drop it off at any Commerce branch, and we'll send you, free of charge, your supply of personalized Gold Cheques.

On the attached application form it says "I will be bound by the terms of the Commerce Gold Cheques Agreement and will be liable for the amount of any Gold Cheques drawn by the Authorized user." Nowhere on the application form do they say what the Commerce Gold Cheques Agreement is. You could be agreeing to anything for all you know.

But what the customer does know about Gold Cheques is bad enough. He is agreeing to pay 18 percent interest immediately on any cheque he writes. It is being charged exactly like a cash advance on a Chargex card. This makes no sense because one can make purchases on Chargex and pay no interest for up to two months.

The Commerce claims it introduced this service for people to buy at stores that do not accept Chargex. But that is no reason to charge interest immediately. This is convenience at a very high price.

Joint Accounts

Many couples have chequing accounts on which both may write cheques. This certainly can be a sound way to handle household expenses to which each party contributes —providing he and she are both responsible about its use. That is the flaw in the use of joint accounts.

Like many couples, Sally and Arthur Hennessy (not their real names) opened a joint account when they rented an apartment and set up housekeeping together. At the end of each month, both deposited $300 into the account and each month they made payments for rent, utilities, and food out of it. Then Arthur lost $500 playing poker and covered his losses with a cheque on the account. Sally was furious but there was nothing she could do.

Far too many people have found out too late that a joint account is just that—an account on which all the people who can sign cheques on it can write cheques on that account for any amount. The only way to prevent irresponsible use of an account like this is to require that all people with access to the account sign every cheque. Sally and Arthur would therefore have to cosign each cheque; a cheque would not be valid without another signature. This would avoid problems such as the one that follows.

Transfers from Other Accounts

Alice Thomas is a public health nurse who thought she handled her money carefully, but she fell into one bad trap. She had her own chequing account in a bank in addition to a joint account with her husband. The joint account was used to pay household bills, while the other account was for her personal needs. The couple separated and her husband stopped putting money into the joint account. That didn't stop him from writing cheques on the joint account, though, and it quickly became overdrawn. The bank then transferred money from Alice's personal account to the joint account to cover the cheques written on it.

She protested to the manager but he told her the bank had the power to do this. All she could do now was to take her signature off the joint account before her husband wrote any more cheques. Until she did that, the bank had the right of set-off.

Pre-authorized Methods of Payment

Consumers often find that a convenient way to make such payments as their monthly mortgage payments is to authorize the bank in advance to deduct these at a regular time. This is far more convenient than having to write a cheque each month, providing the customer remembers to deposit sufficient money in the account to cover the cheque.

Consumers should watch for the bank withdrawing money from their accounts earlier than it is authorized to do so. This practice can easily overdraw the account and lead to paying service charges or interest penalties. If it is found that the bank has withdrawn money prematurely, put up a good fight. A customer of the Bank of Montreal, Graham Qualtrough, collected $527.71 in costs and damages because on eight separate occasions the bank had taken his mortgage payments out of his current account before they were due. This action overdrew the account because Qualtrough deposited sufficient funds to cover the payments only when the payments were due. But by with-drawing money before they were authorized to, the bank claimed there were insufficient funds in the account and charged the customer $4.00 each time.

Qualtrough did not get the settlement easily, however. He started off by complaining to the mortgage department in Montreal in July, moved up to the presidential level in August, and kept up a lively correspondence with the head office and with his bank manager in Vancouver until No-vember. By then the bank had agreed to pay him interest at the savings account rate on his money for the time it had been pre-empted, but Qualtrough did not feel that this was sufficient compensation for his time, effort, and out-of-pocket expenses. He filed a claim in small debts court in late November for $527.71, including $250 for general damages and $150 for loss of income while fighting his case. The balance was for lost interest, service charges, sec-retarial services, postage, and stationery. The bank settled for the full amount because he had a good case and the lawyer's fees would have eaten that much up no matter who won.

According to an article in the Vancouver *Sun,*

> Gene Nesmith, the bank's senior vice-president in B.C., con-ceded the bank had made a mistake in deducting the mortgage payments too early and said he regrets the delays in corre-spondence with Qualtrough.
>
> "Technically we were in breach of the contract we had with him. We had no business doing what we did," Nesmith said. "He went to a lot of bother to demonstrate that to us. He had a point. Rather than go to court and spend his money and ours, we decided to settle."
>
> He added it would have cost the bank more in lawyer's fees if it decided to go to court and Qualtrough might have shown that damages had been caused to him.
>
> Asked how frequently it happens that mortgage payments

are taken out of accounts before the due date, Nesmith admitted: "You can be sure at regular intervals mistakes are made."

But he said the number of times it occurred in Qualtrough's case would be unusual.

He added that it was the bank's misfortune if Qualtrough had "put one over on the bank" by overestimating the amount he should receive but noted "only he can be the judge of that."[6]

Endorsing a Cheque "For Deposit Only"

Customers of banks often sign a cheque "For deposit only in Account ⫞85, John Smith" when they ask another person to deposit it in the bank. Signed this way, the cheque cannot be cashed by anyone else. This type of endorsement locks the cheque into the collection system of the bank.

That is what the person endorsing the cheque intended to do. But doing this can produce a result that is far from the original intention. It gives the bank the power to sue you for the money if the person who wrote the cheque stops payment or if the endorsement was forged.

The "Action Line" column in the Vancouver *Province* reported on the type of problem that someone can get into through forged endorsements.

> There are probably about 10 others who are in the same boat I am. About a month or so ago, a group of others and I were befriended by a man who came regularly to the pub where we drink. He sat with us, bought rounds of beer and played some pool with the group.
>
> One day he asked me to lend him $25, which I did. A week later he handed me his pay cheque from a fish company and asked if I would go to my bank and cash it for him since he didn't have any identification with him. I did so and gave him the $480.40, out of which he paid the $25 he owed me.
>
> A week later my bank charged my account with the $480.40

and cleared out my savings. The pay cheque had been returned by the Bank of B.C., from where it had been drawn,
because the cheque was stolen and the signature was forged.

I since have learned from the police that 42 blank company
cheques had been stolen from the fish company and 10 of
them had been cashed by unsuspecting persons like myself.
Neither the bank nor the fish company had ever known the
cheques were stolen. It wasn't until another break-in had occurred at the plant a couple of weeks later that the theft was
discovered. The Bank of B.C. returned all the cheques with incorrect signatures on them.

I have been everywhere, to the police, the company and the
bank. They all tell me that I am out of luck. Normally I would
have taken this experience as a part of life but the money I
had saved was to pay for a trip to Italy, where I was born.
(Tony La Chimea, Vancouver)[7]

"Action Line" solved this particular problem and Mr.
Chimea was able to pack his bags for Italy. Their first
request for help to the Bank of B.C. produced only a letter
of sympathy from its head office and "the hope that justice
will eventually be served." That was no help but fortunately a lawyer provided a new angle. The bank was treat-
ing the cheque as though the endorsement by Chimea was
forged while in fact it was the signature of the signing
officer of the fish company that was forged. In this kind of
situation, the bank is expected to know its customers and
detect the forgery within twenty-four hours. If it does not,
it loses all recourse and is liable for the amount of the
cheque. The Bank of B.C. consequently changed its position, and paid off all ten cheques.

The Thirty-day Rule

Banking institutions have a Thirty-day Rule which a customer agrees to when he signs a signature card opening up
the account.

Metropolitan Trust asks its depositors to sign an agreement which includes this stipulation:

> With respect to each account maintained by the Depositor with the Trust Company, the Depositor will examine each statement of account and relative cheques and vouchers and within thirty days of the delivery of the same (or, if the Trust Company is directed to forward such statements, cheques and vouchers by mail to the Depositor, within thirty days of the date of mailing of the same) will notify the Trust Company in writing of any errors, irregularities or omissions therein and therefrom and upon the expiration of the said period of thirty days the account as kept by the Trust Company shall be conclusive evidence without any further proof that, save as to any errors, irregularities or omissions previously notified to the Trust Company as aforesaid and save as to payments made on forged or unauthorized endorsements, the account contains all credits that should be contained therein and all the entries therein are correct and subject to the above exception, the Trust Company shall be free from all claims in respect of the account.

Stripped of the legalese, this means that you had better get with it within the thirty days of the mailing of your bank statement or suffer the consequences, as happened to a member of the Retail Merchants Association in Vancouver.

He was busy opening a new store selling men's clothing and did not discover that his account had been incorrectly charged with $10,000 until after the thirty-day limit had elapsed. The bank refused to return the $10,000 to his account until he told the story on an open-line radio show. Within an hour the bank had contacted him and agreed to return the $10,000 as well as pay his legal fees.

The wording of this agreement can also be deceiving with regard to consumer's rights or the bank's policy on disputed accounts. For example, few consumers realize that most deposit institutions will absorb losses paid out of consumer's accounts through forgeries, adverse claims, or

material alterations. In addition, consumers do have some
legal rights even if the account has not been verified. But
this fact is one that, as one commentator said, "the banks
do not customarily advertise: Every month we figure out
how much we owe you. If you don't like our figures, you'd
better complain quick; otherwise we won't accept your
proof; that's tough but otherwise, we couldn't make the
system work."[8]

Should the Banking Institutions Pay Interest on Chequing Accounts?

In January 1981, there was $3.9 billion in personal
chequing accounts and $12.7 billion in other types of de-
mand accounts in the Canadian banks. That is a lot of
money earning no interest. Many people believe that it
should not be used free of charge by the banks. The banks
do not agree, of course, because they like free money except when they provide it for their cash reserves with the
Bank of Canada. Then they think they should receive interest.

The Canadian banks are not legally restricted from paying interest on chequing accounts but they have fought the
idea for a long time. They capitulated a number of years
ago to large depositors with demand deposits over
$100,000, but the average person is not in that league.

In the United States before the depression, there was a
tradition of paying interest on chequing accounts and
American banks are working back to this stage. *Consumer
Reports* agrees that small accounts are much less profitable
than big accounts but adds that the smaller accounts can
be accumulated for loaning out at 10 to 18 percent a year
to generate profits for the bank.

"Back in the early part of the century," according to

Consumer Reports, "banks acknowledged the expense-producing character of chequing accounts by paying interest on these deposits." The practice was stopped by the Banking Act of 1933, passed during the Great Depression. (According to the conventional economic wisdom of the period, stiff competition for these funds forced banks to bid interest rates up so high that the increased cost contributed to the bank failures in the late 1920s and early 1930s.) Now, instead of attracting depositors by paying interest for the use of funds in chequing accounts, banks pay an "implicit" rate of interest (estimated to be about 3 percent) through such interest substitutes as promotional gifts, "free" chequing, longer hours, extra branches, and investment advice.

Most economists today believe the prohibition on interest payments for chequing accounts was misguided and that the practice had no bearing on bank failures. Nevertheless, the question today is usually not "how much the balance deposited in a chequing account will earn, but how much the chequing account will cost."[9]

Americans now have chequable savings accounts, called NOW for Negotiable Order of Withdrawal. The rates of interest and charges vary widely so that in some cases the return is quite similar to the savings-chequing accounts at Canadian banks.

Other devices have been introduced in the fiercely competitive American banking scene which in effect mean that customers get interest on all of their money held by a bank. It is generally done through an automatic transfer service that moves money from an interest-paying savings account to a non-interest-paying chequing account whenever the customer wants to write a cheque.

This is done in Canada on a routine basis for select customers who request this service. It is not a generally advertised benefit though, and most consumers are unaware that it can be done. Some credit unions are now providing this service and it would be a real benefit to consumers if the practice became more widespread.

If cash transfers like this become widespread, demand deposits will drop as a percentage of total personal savings even faster than they are now. This has intriguing implications for governments trying to control the economy through manipulation of the money supply.

If the government is trying to control the money supply and hence the economy by manipulating chequing accounts, it could get a very false impression by looking only at changes in the size of chequing accounts at a time when billions of dollars in savings accounts are really being used as chequing accounts.

9

Savings on Your Savings

"Who benefits from the economic insecurity that has Canadians stashing away their money in bigger bunches than ever before? The banks do, that's who," according to the Vancouver *Sun*.[1]

Canadians have been saving record amounts in recent years because of, or in spite of, inflation. Historically we save about 5 percent of our income after taxes but this savings rate has more than doubled to 12 percent in recent years and it is three times as high as the American savings rate.

By the third quarter 1980, Canadians had $259 billion tucked away in financial institutions and basic savings vehicles—$77.6 billion of it in chartered banks, $33.4 billion in trust companies, and $27.9 billion in credit unions. In addition, Canadians had invested $8.7 billion in mortgage companies, almost $3.4 billion in investment funds, $4.3 billion in government savings banks, $47.6 billion in trusteed pension plans, $16.3 billion in Canada Savings Bonds, $31.2 billion in life insurance, and $8.6 billion in other funds. Some of this huge sum was invested sensibly, a lot of it was not.

Why do consumers save these huge sums? They accumulate money for several basic reasons—an underlying sense of insecurity, the fear of inflation, and planning for the future all play their part in the process. In any case, one must handle his savings intelligently and make the most of them.

To do this, decide first of all when, if ever, you are going to need the money. Most people have three different time spans that they should plan around:

1.—a rainy day—it can happen any time. That means having some money safely socked away which you can turn into cash quickly and easily.
2.—a planned expenditure. That means accumulating a definite sum of money during a definite period of time and being able to turn it safely into cash at the end of that time.
3.—a long-term plan to provide investment income, retirement income, or a general increase in your financial well-being. This requires the consistent accumulation of savings and the sound investment of these funds.

Rainy-day money should be invested in a way that is relatively secure and highly liquid like Canada Savings Bonds, term deposits, or a bond investment fund. It should not be put into a savings account because it is too easy to draw it out and spend it, and the interest rate is usually lower.

Saving for a planned expenditure, provided it is less than a year away, can be done with a savings account because any amount of money can be deposited at any time or withdrawn at any time. Be sure that the best type of savings account is chosen.

Long-term saving should include some of these possibilities—a pension plan, a tax shelter such as an RHOSP, a tax deferral scheme like a RRSP, investment funds, bonds, stocks, gold, and real estate. The mix will be different for everyone.

Choosing the Right Savings Account

There are almost as many different types of savings accounts as there are different financial institutions. The common denominator of them all is that they pay interest. What separates them is first of all how they pay that interest. It can make a world of difference. Savings accounts also differ in the ways that money can be withdrawn from them. Technically speaking, money can be withdrawn from a savings account only on seven days' notice, but this requirement is seldom, if ever, enforced.

Obviously, the way in which your interest is calculated can make a real difference in the amount you earn on a savings account.

Calculating interest every six months on the minimum monthly balance is the worst way, from the consumer's point of view. Interest calculated and compounded on the daily balance is the best deal. This is quite apparent if you compare the different ways that interest is computed and credited to an account.

Start with calculating the simple interest for a year. Multiply the amount in the savings account by the quoted interest rate. A $10,000 savings account receiving 8 percent interest would earn in a year

$$\$10,000 \times 0.08 = \$800$$

A slightly better return on your money is obtained if the interest is calculated on the minimum balance every six months so that the depositor receives interest on the interest in the second half of the year.

After six months, the account receives interest of

$$\$10,000 \times \frac{0.08}{2} = \$400$$

The account will now have this much money in it:

$10,000 + \$400$ interest $= \$10,400$

At the end of the year, the interest payment will be

$$\$10,400 \times \frac{0.08}{2} = \$416$$

The account now has $10,400 + \$416 = \$10,816$. As a result of receiving interest semiannually instead of annually, the depositor has increased his return from $800 to $816. The only drawback in this type of account is that the interest is calculated on the minimum balance over a six-month period. Drop down to a dollar balance in the account for one day but leave $10,000 in the account for the rest of the six months and you will get $.04 in interest.

Now compare those two types of accounts with an account where the interest is calculated on the daily balance. Here is an account where the daily balance varies quite a bit throughout the month.

DAILY INTEREST SAVINGS ACCOUNT
PAYING INTEREST AT 9 PERCENT A YEAR

| | | MONTHLY INTEREST | |
| | BALANCE | On Minimum | On Daily |
DATE	IN ACCOUNT	Balance	Balance
MAY 1	$ 300		
5	1,200		5 days $0.37
18	800		13 days 3.85
28	3,000		10 days 1.97
			3 days 2.92
31		31 days $2.29	31 days 8.41

The balance in this account varied over the month from a minimum of $300 to a maximum of $3,000. If the interest at 9 percent had been calculated on the minimum amount on any one day—$300—it would have been only $2.29. If the interest had been calculated on the daily balance, it would have been $8.41, nearly four times as much. This is obviously the only kind of account to have if the daily balance in your savings accounts varies substantially during the month.

Choosing a savings account that pays the highest effective rate of interest is important to consumers, but the significance of the different ways of calculating interest is often not apparent to them. They cannot make reasonable comparisons between the rates of return on different savings accounts because the method of computing interest on deposits is not standardized.

The Consumers' Association of Canada believes that financial institutions should have to do this. In their view this is "a grave omission, which leaves consumers vulnerable to enormous confusion in the face of competing claims about interest rates that are themselves calculated according to different methods. For example, there are probably very few consumers who are sophisticated enough to discern the difference between (a) 6% compounded semiannually and calculated on the basis of average daily balances and (b) 6% compounded monthly using the minimum monthly balance method. In not specifying a uniform interest computation procedure, the regulations do nothing to alleviate this type of confusion."[2]

Many American banks, the Bank of British Columbia, and some Canadian credit unions and trust companies have paid interest on the daily balances in savings accounts for years but our big national Canadian banks said, "No way—it is too difficult and too complicated." The federal government even introduced legislation four years ago making it compulsory, but the powerful Canadian Bankers' Association mounted another successful pressure lobby and got the law scrubbed. Then, all of a sudden, these banking geniuses found out how to calculate daily interest. Years of preparing and presenting elaborate briefs to parliamentary committees went down the drain. Every bank now pays interest on a daily basis on its savings accounts.

On the surface that looks like a victory for the consumer, but wait before you shout any hosannas. You may have forgotten the old adage about always reading the fine print.

These new savings accounts are not all they might seem on the surface. There are traps for the unwary. The rate of interest varies and it may be paid monthly or semiannually. It is also about ¾ of 1 percent less than the rate on a regular savings account. The bank may require a minimum monthly balance before you get any interest. There may be service charges on withdrawals. A few allow chequing. The net result is that you could end up paying more in service charges and lost interest with one of these accounts if you do not analyze it carefully for your particular needs.

Just who benefits, the bank or the consumer, will depend on the "smartness" or "efficiency" of the consumer, according to a study prepared by an investment dealer, Burns Fry Limited, in August 1979. They pointed out that individuals had $27 billion in nonchequable savings accounts but they earned no interest on about $1.9 billion of this money because their minimum monthly balance fell below their average monthly balance on 7 percent of these total savings accounts.

The study goes on to point out:

... given a 9½% daily average rate and a perfectly intelligent world any depositor whose minimum monthly balance was less than 92½% of his average monthly balance would switch into a daily average savings account which would produce a benefit to the consumer/depositor and a net increase in interest cost to the bank. However not all depositors are financially sophisticated. In fact with the likely plethora of plans to be available from banks and near banks, each with its unique characteristics, the consumer is likely to be quite confused. In addition the imposition of high withdrawal and transfer charges will make it too costly for the low value/high transaction depositor to convert into a daily average interest savings account.

The firm also estimated that the cost to the banks of introducing these new accounts would be about $25 to $40 million a year, or about 3 percent of their earnings. Consumers, on the other hand, will benefit only if they study their options carefully.

The Passbook

A passbook is the little book that records the ins and outs of your savings account. You pass it to the teller, the teller writes it up or snaps in a message from the computer and passes it back to you. It passes to and fro between you and the teller and this action has legal significance. The passbook states the amount in the account and its proper function, as a result of this passing around, is to provide a conclusive and unquestionable record of the transactions between the bank and the customer.

Charges for Closing Out a Savings Account Too Quickly

Banking institutions like consumers to leave their money in savings accounts for a minimum time of at least six months. Because it costs them money to open an account and to close an account, they believe that they will lose money if the account is closed out too quickly. That is the reason why some banks charge a consumer for closing out a savings account or pay no interest if you have not left the money there for a reasonable time.

The Bank of Nova Scotia charged an account $5.00 because less than $50 was left in it for less than one month. Another customer was charged $1.00 by the Bank of Montreal because the account had been closed in less than three months. The Commerce charged $1.00 because the account had been kept open for less than six months. The Royal Bank charged $2.50 because the account was closed within a month.

What Other Ways Are There to Save in the Banking System?

Savings accounts are not the only way to accumulate savings in the banking system. There are term deposits, savings certificates, and guaranteed investment certificates. These alternatives generally have the advantage of providing a rate of interest higher than that paid on savings accounts, although often at a penalty. In some cases, the holder of these securities cannot get his money back for a certain time period. In others, the interest rate is reduced if the security is cashed prematurely.

Term deposits are sold by banks, trust companies, and credit unions for a number of days until the deposit matures and the money is returned to the customer. This time period can vary from a few days to six years. They can be bought for any number of days from 30 to 364, providing you invest a minimum of $5,000. These deposits can be cashed before they mature but the interest rate will be reduced usually by ¼ of 1 percent. Term deposits can also be bought at the banks for terms of one to six years, with a minimum of $1,000. These are also cashable before maturity, subject to a reduction from about ½ of 1 percent to 2 percent in the interest rate.

The banks sell savings certificates that mature in six years in amounts as low as $10. These are also cashable before maturity at a lower rate of interest.

Guaranteed investment certificates are sold by trust companies. They can be bought for terms of less than a year from some companies, but most GICs have terms of one, two, three, four, or five years. Most of them cannot be cashed before maturity unless the certificate holder dies. The holder is essentially locked into the investment and, for most consumers, this is a poor deal. They should either get a much higher rate to compensate them for this disadvantage or put their money elsewhere.

10

The Red Convertible Loan

The Bank of Montreal sends out the most heartwarming letters. One that came in a consumer's mail said:

Dear Customer:
Just a brief note to let you know that interest rates on our personal life insured loans range from 13% to 15%.

If you have any loan needs now or in the future, please feel free to call me and discuss the matter. We assure you that any application you might make will receive favourable consideration.

Yours truly,
xxxxxxxxxxxxxxx
Consumer Loans Clerk

Coincidentally she also received a notice from Master Charge to say that they had increased her credit limit by a substantial amount. A lot of people are having the same experience these days. The banks are coming to them with enticing offers of quick loans and easy credit, even though none of these people have asked for a loan or for increased credit. It is all part of the "red convertible" syndrome.

From 1960 to 1970 consumers increased their outstanding credit balances threefold to $10.5 billion. In the next ten years consumers took on debt even faster as their credit balances rose 4.1 times to $43 billion. And who got the major share of this huge increase in loans? The chartered banks, thanks to the change in the 1967 Bank Act removing the 6 percent ceiling on interest rates charged on personal loans. The banks hold $16 billion in demand deposits on which they pay little or no interest and now they can loan most of this money out at whatever interest rate the market will bear. That makes the banks with their cheap money very strong competitors for the trust companies and the finance companies which pay dearly to raise the money to make loans. It is little wonder then that the sales finance companies and the consumer loan companies barely managed to keep ahead of the game. Now you can understand why the finance companies want to become banks and why trust companies try to be banks. The credit unions have been the only real competitors for this lucrative business.

CREDIT BALANCES OF CONSUMERS
(IN MILLIONS OF DOLLARS)

Year	Sales Finance and Consumer Loan Companies	Chartered Banks Personal Loans	Trust and Loan Companies	Credit Unions	Other	Total
1960	1,378	857	..	433	1,353	4,021
1970	2,851	4,663	..	1,493	1,501	10,508
1980	2,664	28,790	1,527	6,415	3,631	43,027
% Increase:						
1960–70	10%	444%	..	245%	11%	161%
1970–80	−6.6%	517%	..	330%	142%	309%

Source: Statistics Canada, *Consumer Credit*

The friendly banker is obviously doing very nicely, but is the consumer faring as well? Credit that is easily available lets most of us have many of the material advantages of our society, but it leaves unanswered some serious questions. The major one centres around the problem of the overcommitted debtor—the consumer who has been encouraged by slick advertising and easy credit terms to buy a red convertible when he should be taking the bus. Another is that of people who are left out of our free-spending society because they don't fit the lender's mould of the desirable credit risk. Lastly, there are the ever-present pitfalls for the consumer that could be avoided by greater care on his part or better lending practices by the banking system.

A consumer should follow a careful plan when shopping for a loan, read and understand the fine print on the loan agreement, and learn his rights and responsibilities. If you do not do this, you may end up getting the wrong kind of loan, paying too much for it, or paying too stiff a penalty if you cannot meet the payments.

Shopping for a Loan

Harry Johnston is a man in his mid-twenties with a wife, three-month-old son, and a steady job that pays about $15,000 a year. He had never borrowed money and was not very sure of how he should go about it. But he felt he had to tackle this problem because he and his wife wanted to buy a car.

The car dealer was willing to finance the car but Harry was not sure that this was the thing to do. The window of every bank, trust company, and credit union that he passed on the way to work offered to loan him money, but he had never talked to a bank manager and he was intimidated by the thought of it.

Somehow he gathered up his courage and walked up to a clerk in his bank to ask about the car loan. The clerk took him in to see the manager and this is where he nearly blew it. He was so flustered that he could not remember such simple facts about himself as how much he had earned in the past year.

Some bank managers, when they meet a customer like Harry, seem to get a perverse pleasure out of creating the atmosphere that Stephen Leacock described so well in his famous story, "My Financial Career."

> When I go into a bank I get rattled. The clerks rattle me; the wickets rattle me; the sight of the money rattles me; everything rattles me.
>
> The moment I cross the threshold of a bank and attempt to transact business there, I become an irresponsible idiot.[1]

Harry was luckier than Leacock. The bank manager understood Harry and helped him make the loan application and quoted him a rate. The deal was signed, sealed, and delivered within twenty-four hours. Harry had his "red convertible loan"—and his red convertible, providing he kept the payments up. He also has a vague idea of what interest rate he is paying, and of course he knows how much he must pay each month.

But what Harry does not know is a lot more than what he does know. He does not know what the fine print in his loan agreement means. He does not know that he could have got a lower interest rate from that bank or from other banks. He does not know the penalty he would pay if he decided to retire the loan before it was due. And he does not know what will happen to his red convertible if he is laid off work and misses a few payments. These are the most important things to keep in mind when you are looking for a loan. The next time Harry may be a lot smarter.

Bargain with Your Banker

There is no such thing as a set rate in consumer lending. There are only rates around which you bargain. Approach every banker as you would a merchant in an oriental bazaar. The merchant-banker has something he wants to sell and he wants to make as much money as he can on the trade. But he knows that he cannot make any money unless he makes a trade. Better a shaved profit margin than no deal at all.

Mike Grenby of the Vancouver *Sun* quoted two bank managers in his syndicated column whom he questioned on the subject of bargaining for consumer loans. Gene Nesmith, senior vice-president of the Bank of Montreal for B.C., said that their "managers always have the authority to set an interest rate to beat or at least match the competition. Of course, it depends on the applicant, too." The Royal Bank's retail marketing manager, Don Morris, confirmed a similar policy because "each branch always has the discretion to change rates if necessary to keep business."[2]

The clue here is that you have to bargain for lower rates. Start by finding out what the competition is offering. Then make it perfectly clear to the bank manager that you have absolutely no qualms about taking your business elsewhere. You would be amazed at the number of people who feel a sense of obligation or loyalty to a particular bank when all that bank has done is cash their cheques and held their savings for years while charging them exactly what they charge everybody else. (It is an entirely different matter if the bank has provided special services for a customer, but that is a subject for a later chapter.)

You must realize also that the bank manager is most unlikely to quote the lowest rate that he is prepared to offer. Why should he say he will loan money at 11 percent when you might just be dumb enough to pay 15 percent? You have to ask for it. And you will have to provide a few good reasons why you should get it.

The first reason is that you can get the money cheaper across the street. The second reason is that you are a good credit risk. Be prepared to document this with proof of income and a statement of your net worth (all your assets and liabilities). Point out that you are a good customer of the bank and you expect that you will be doing more business there. You may be considering a mortgage to buy a house or a Registered Retirement Savings Plan. Banks like providing "a total service." And do not count on remembering all these points when you are seated across the table from the bank manager. Write them down carefully and take the list with you when you go to the bank to negotiate your loan.

The Loan Agreement

Consumers who take out a loan from a banking institution are required to sign a loan agreement. Usually, this is a standard form which leaves you with little or no opportunity to bargain for better terms. Until very recently, most consumers never read this form thoroughly enough to understand what it meant. For that matter, most consumers could not understand it no matter how many times they read it because it was printed in fine type and written in convoluted sentences with all the interminable whereases and whereifs and disclaimers that lawyers use to disguise the real purpose of a contract. Here, the real purpose of the

How to Compare Loan Rates and Terms

Type of Loan	Annual Interest Rate	Costs Included	Costs Not Included
CHARTERED BANK			
General Purpose Personal Loan	12–15%	Life Insurance	Disability Insurance
Demand Loan	Prime rate and up.		Life and Disability Insurance
Credit Card	18%		Life and Disability Insurance
Cash Advance on Credit Card	18%		Life and Disability Insurance
Investment Loan	12–15%	Life Insurance	Disability Insurance
TRUST COMPANY			
General Purpose Personal Loan	12–15%	Life Insurance	Disability Insurance
Demand Loan	12–13½%		Life and Disability Insurance
FINANCE COMPANY			
Conditional Sales Contract	18–24%		Life and Disability Insurance
SMALL LOAN COMPANY	Up to 24% on less than $1,500		Life and Disability Insurance
DEPARTMENT STORE CREDIT	18–30%		Life and Disability Insurance
CREDIT UNION	12–12½%	May have Life Insurance	Disability Insurance

loan agreement is to put all the power in the hands of the banks.

Provincial governments have tried during the last ten years to bring in laws that offer some protection to borrowers, but the game is still weighted heavily in favour of the lender. "Even though these protective laws exist, there still remains a fundamental inequity between the parties in

Advantages	Disadvantages
Flexible prepayment without penalty; 24-hr. service; may be interest rebate up to 100% financing.	No disability coverage over age 64 or if not working full time; may demand cosigning by spouse or other guarantor; may demand chattel mortgage.
Rate may be lower.	Requires cashable security; rate fluctuates with prime rate; subject to immediate call. Expensive.
Available up to credit limit at any time; interest deferred 30–60 days; have legal title to purchases; cannot be subject to seizure.	
Quick access to cash.	Interest starts immediately.
Tax deduction on interest.	May be maximum of $10,000; may require monthly payments.
No prepayment penalty; may use simple interest calculation; no legal or appraisal fees if secured by house.	Same as bank.
	Same as bank demand loan.
Point of Purchase Financing.	May charge investigation fees; late payment charges; early payout charges; may charge interest in advance; you do not have legal possession until you pay for it.
	Rates may be very high; prepayment charges on unregulated loans.
Convenient; merchant does not have right to seizure.	Cost.
Use simple interest calculation; no penalty for prepayment.	Must join credit union.

a consumer credit agreement," according to Allan Parker in the *Credit Law and Bankruptcy Handbook.*

The advantage in such an agreement clearly rests with the grantor. The grantor has financial resources, knowledge, and experience far beyond the average individual. With superior financial resources, the creditor has ready access to the courts to enforce an agreement, while a debtor may be unable to advance a valid defence because he or she cannot afford a lawyer. Some creditors may use their knowledge and experience to unfair or even illegal ends in collecting from a debtor who is behind in a payment while at the same time playing on the fear and ignorance of the debtor.[3]

The British Columbia government fought the banks over this point. Minister of Consumer Services Phyllis Young started the battle in 1974 when she told businesses to check all their contract forms and other documents to be sure that the language used in these forms did not misrepresent the consumer's legal rights.

The banks took the lofty stand that they did not have to respect, let alone follow, provincial laws because they were above them. In their view, they only had to adhere to federal laws because they were regulated by the Bank Act of the federal government and that government was the only one that had the power to regulate banks. The federal government showed that it had no intention of regulating the banks in this regard.

When there had been no progress for three years, the next Minister of Consumer and Corporate Affairs, Rafe Mair, took up the battle. He complained to federal Minister of Finance, Jean Chrétien, with no success. Chrétien claimed that the policy of the banks was to abide by provincial laws but, as Mair clearly showed in this letter, the banks were in fact violating four laws of British Columbia that are designed to protect consumers, the Sale of Goods Act, Conditional Sales Act, Bills of Sale Act, and Debt Collection Act.

The major violation of these acts by the banks was their practice of "seizing and suing." A borrower would get behind on his car payments, the bank would seize the car, sell it at a mark-down price, and then sue the borrower for any debt remaining.

B.C. law was designed to prevent this kind of situation

by saying that the bank could either seize the car or sue for the debt, but not both. Nevertheless, the banks specifically drafted a loan agreement for B.C. borrowers that claimed that they could both seize and sue.

Mair complained to Chrétien in a letter dated November 22, 1977:

> I am writing in reply to your letter of October 14th, in part to express my profound disappointment and, in part, to point out the errors in fact that underlie your reply.
>
> First, while you say that it "is the policy of most of the banks to make every effort to comply with the Provincial legislation," the bald fact is that "policy" differs very much from "fact," and quite clearly, the banks are not telling you the truth. As an example, I attach a chattel mortgage document currently in use by the Canadian Imperial Bank of Commerce, specifically drafted for British Columbia (Form 422 B.C.-74). This document and others in use by the banks categorically or by implication exclude the application of these Provincial Acts:
>
> 1. Sale of Goods Act: re: purported waiver of statutory implied conditions and warranties despite the provision of S.21A.
> 2. Conditional Sales Act: the seize or sue provision.
> 3. Bills of Sale Act: the seize or sue provision and other specific provisions notably Ss.22A, B, C & D.
> 4. Debt Collection Act: specifically S.14 (i), (f) & (g).
>
> Other banks are using similar forms. In our opinion, they are, by misstating the rights of consumers, representing "that a consumer transaction involves or does not involve rights, remedies or obligations" when that representation is deceptive or misleading, and thus, are in contravention of our Trade Practices Act.

Mair also complained about a form of guarantee being used by a number of banks. He specifically mentioned that it was used by the Bank of Montreal and the Bank of Nova Scotia. According to Mair's letter,

. . . consumers are asked to sign [this form] as a guarantee of a specific loan, but which is, in fact, a promise to permanently underwrite any loan with the specific institution that may be undertaken by the primary borrower at any time in the future up to the amount signed for or the "amount" may be unstated and therefore, limitless. We take the view that in using these forms in a consumer transaction, banks are acting unconscionably and we will be prosecuting under the Trade Practices Act in an appropriate case, and also considering civil proceedings for a declaration of injunction.

The B.C. government did follow up on its demands for better lending practices by the banks, and several cases showed how effective they were. An enforcement report from the Consumer and Corporate Affairs Department said:

The Canadian Imperial Bank of Commerce dropped an action against a consumer in a case involving provincial "seize or sue" provisions, after the Director of Trade Practices assumed conduct of the case. When the consumers failed to make their payments as scheduled, the bank repossessed the truck and camper, and initiated a lawsuit against one consumer for the difference between the amount owing and the amount recovered in resale. The Director of Trade Practices entered the case because B.C. law states that a creditor may either "seize or sue"—but not both—for the balance owing on goods.

In his consumer column in the *Province,* Lorne Parton's comment on this decision was, "You think the banks built all those skyscrapers on Mary's smile and Anne Murray's song?"[4]

Some of the banks eventually simplified their loan forms. With great fanfare, the Bank of Nova Scotia announced in April 1979, after nearly five years of government requests, that they were introducing simplified consumer loan forms in British Columbia. The bank claims that it took them three years to develop a form that had nontechnical language, larger type, subheadings, and colour; either the bank has the most inefficient lawyers in the country or, as many people suspect, there was a lot of foot-dragging in this business.

Nevertheless, the simplified loan form is here and it is a great improvement. Take this example of before and after:

Before:	*After:*
The mortgagor shall continue to keep the property free and clear of all liens and encumbrances and shall at all times use the property strictly in accordance with all statutes, by-laws and regulations from time to time in force.	You will keep the property clear of all legal claims against it except ours.

The bank said the form was being introduced first in B.C. and would become available in the other provinces during the next year. The Nova Scotia claims to be the first Canadian bank to introduce these forms, although several major American banks have them.

This whole business is just another one of the ways in which the federal government neglects the welfare of the average bank customer when it comes time to consider the laws or regulations affecting banking practise. As Allan Fotheringham pointed out in *Maclean's,*

> What brings the bile juices to a boil is the fact that Ottawa now has a chance via the decennial review of the Bank Act to do something about the cozy cartel and, at last, one of the provinces has stepped in on behalf of the consumer to describe the essential character of bank practices. B.C. Minister of Consumer and Corporate Affairs Rafe Mair, a Social Credit millionaire lawyer who is hardly a radical, says chartered banks "flagrantly break" the B.C. law every day with shady consumer lending practices that involve threats, deceit and outright

blackmail. Beneath those six-piece serge suits, there beats the avarice of used car salesmen in loud checks.

Mair, detailing the slippery dealings that defy six separate B.C. laws, says, "In terms of the nature of violations, the Bank of Nova Scotia is worst. The Canadian Imperial Bank of Commerce is second because it's biggest in B.C. and affects most people." This is the same Scotiabank that has refused to join other members of the cozy cartel in killing those seducing "red convertible" come-on ads that so encourage Canadians to rush into debt. The Scotiabank we know was a vehicle in the Gulf Oil bribery scandals, laundering Gulf money through a phony Nassau account with the result that such delightful people as South Korea's Park Chung Hee could be bribed with one million dollars in Gulf bribes. It was arranged through the late William K. Whiteford, who came to Gulf from Toronto, where he had been a Scotiabank director for 15 years.[5]

The implication of all this is obvious. Watch what you are signing; read it thoroughly; ask questions, and sign nothing that is not crystal clear to you. You are not dealing with the Salvation Army.

The Real Cost of Borrowing

You pay to borrow money and sometimes you pay more than you should or more than you think you are paying. Lenders of money have a lot of fancy ways to get that extra amount out of unsuspecting borrowers. They may state the rate or amount of interest in a misleading way or they may add on all sorts of extra charges for credit investigation, insurance, or registration fees on collateral.

The federal government introduced a bill in 1977 called the Borrowers' and Depositors' Protection Act which was supposed to deal with most aspects of this problem. It was primarily designed to provide adequate disclosure of interest rates and costs for consumers along the line of the

Truth-in-Lending Act in the United States and some of our provincial laws. Basically it would have required that lenders use a uniform method of calculating interest and other costs so that consumers could compare charges between different banking institutions and other lenders.

A soundly written Truth-in-Lending act makes it easier for consumers to choose the least expensive source of any loan. (A look at the chart on pages 138 and 139 shows how this can help.) But lenders do not want to enable consumers to make such comparisons. They fought the Borrowers' Act in every way possible, and as Senator David Croll said, corridors were crawling with lobbyists. When the federal government caved in, the act died a quiet death.

As a sop to consumers, Finance Minister Jean Chrétien brought out some draft regulations in January of 1979 on the calculation and disclosure of the costs of borrowing. They went into effect with the new Bank Act. As almost anything would have been an improvement, these regulations must be regarded as a constructive step. They will impose on the chartered banks and the Quebec savings bank (and *not* on any other lender) a minimum standard of disclosure to the public of most of the costs involved in a loan. But as the Consumers' Association points out, "Unfortunately, as a consumer or bank protection measure, the regulations are regrettably deficient, falling far short of previous government promises to improve the market for consumer borrowing and lending."[6]

Consumers can still be misled or uninformed about the real cost of borrowing. Other consumer lenders do not have to conform to these laws. It remains difficult to make rate comparisons as it is still an acceptable practice to calculate interest and finance charges in different ways.

However, there are straightforward ways of calculating rates of interest. For example, credit unions charge interest on outstanding balances on a monthly basis; other lenders precompute total interest over the life of a loan and then charge the interest either by amortization or by the Rule of 78.

Watch Out for the Rule of 78

Banks and other lenders have often used a controversial method of calculating monthly loan repayments called the Rule of 78, or the sum of the digits method, for calculating monthly payments on consumer loans. The consumer repays part of the principal owing and part of the interest owing each month. The total monthly payment will always be the same but the percentage considered as an interest payment can change by a large amount, depending on how the interest is calculated and on how long the loan is.

Many lenders like to use the Rule of 78 to calculate the breakdown between interest and principal because they will get a larger interest payment at the beginning of the loan, the time when they incur the bulk of their costs in making a loan. The problem for consumers arises when they prepay a loan early. If their loan repayments are calculated using the Rule of 78, the borrower ends up paying a higher rate of interest than he had bargained for.

The origin of the name Rule of 78 is the fact that there are 12 months in a year and, if you assign a number from one to twelve for each month, it adds up to 78. January is 12, February is 11, and so on to 1 for December. Add up $12 + 11 + 10 + 9 + 8 + 7 + 6 + 5 + 4 + 3 + 2 + 1$ and you get 78.

Now calculate the interest you pay on your loan each month in this manner. Multiply the amount you owe by the number for the month and divide by 78.

Using the example of $1,000 borrowed for one year at

12 percent to be repaid in equal monthly instalments of $88.85, with a precomputed interest charge of $66.20 for the total interest cost we see:

Month	Amount Owed	Digit	Interest Payment	Principal Repayment	Balance Owing
Jan.	$1,000	12	$66.20 × $\frac{12}{78}$ = $10.18	$88.85 − $10.18 = $78.67	$921.33
Feb.	$921.33	11	$66.20 × $\frac{11}{78}$ = $9.34	$88.85 − $9.34 = $79.51	$841.82

If the loan is taken out for more than 12 months, the sum of the digits will be more than 78. A loan for 2 years or 24 months will produce a sum of the digits of 300. The first month of the loan will then be 24 and the digit used for the interest calculation for that month will be 24/300.

If a borrower pays off a loan early and interest has been calculated by the Rule of 78, he should receive a rebate of the precomputed interest. But this formula does not produce an accurate rebate and is biased in favour of the lender.

If the loan in the previous example is repaid in two months, the interest rebate should be this amount:

1) Calculate Total Principal and Interest of Loan (monthly payment times the monthly term of the loan)
   $88.85 × 12 = $1,066.20
2) Cost of borrowing is Total Principal and Interest minus Principal
   $1,066.20 − $1,000.00 = $66.20
3) Amount of Rebate is calculated by a formula: Cost of borrowing − [Cost of borrowing × $\frac{\text{Digits of Months Paid}}{\text{Total Sum of Digits}}$]

   or $66.20 − \left($66.20 × \frac{12 + 11}{78} \right) = $46.68

Amount of Money Required to Pay off Loan

Total Principal and Interest	$1,066.20
Less: 2 payments of $88.85 each	177.70
Less: rebate	46.68
Total Repayment	$ 841.82

To see the difference between the Rule of 78 and a simple interest loan, take the example of a loan of $1,000 for a year at 12 percent that you plan to repay with regular monthly payments. If the bank uses a simple interest calculation and you repay it in three months, the interest charge will be $27.63. If the bank used the Rule of 78, the interest charge would now be $28.01, or $.38 more.

That is not enough to hassle a bank manager. The difference between the two interest calculations is not very significant for small amounts borrowed for shorter periods of time. But it does become very important if you are borrowing more than $2,000 for over two years.

Take an actual example where $10,000 was borrowed for 15 years at an annual rate of 13½ percent. Almost 4 years later, more than $10,000 was still owed the bank, even though payments of $5,700 had been made in that time, because the interest charged each month on the loan was more than the monthly payment.

Many banks did not tell their customers about the cost of early prepayment. The excuses they gave for this were interesting. One loan officer said he used to tell customers, "but they let it go in one ear and out the other because their only concern when they borrowed money was to make the specified monthly payments. Customers just do not anticipate prepaying loans."

The new Bank Act will make the use of the Rule of 78 illegal. Interest on consumer loans must be calculated by the actuarial method. Consumers will also have the right to prepay a consumer loan of up to $50,000 at any time with prepayment penalties either limited or prohibited.

With these changes, investment dealer Burns Fry Limited predicts that "the consumer gets the best of all worlds." The lender however is still stuck with the problem of recovering the cost of writing a consumer loan contract. This is about $100 and it must be recovered somehow.

"Considering the banks are still in the business to make a reasonable return," adds Burns Fry,

> . . . and that domestic retail profit margins are at least at a 15-year low (and too low in our opinion to sustain future growth) the obvious answer to us (perhaps not as obvious to politicians) is that banks and other consumer lenders will raise their consumer loan rates across the board to a level that is adequate to offset these additional costs. Of course, the end result is that most people who either do not refinance their consumer loans or those who are not "financially astute" will end up subsidizing the lesser proportion of the population who prepay their loans and/or are "financially astute."[7]

It seems that consumers may not benefit much from these new rules after all.

The Lure of Debt Consolidation

Commercials for finance companies sing of the joys of combining all your little loans into one convenient loan that requires only one cheque each month. But what a cheque! Unless you are able to stretch the payments over a longer time, it will be at least as big as the total of all your previous payments, and it may even be higher because of additional refinancing charges. Bank managers have grave

reservations about such loans. The manager of a branch of
the Bank of Montreal told me that he had stopped making
these kinds of loans because they are not in the best interests of most people. In his experience, a debt consolidation
loan by itself is no solution.

> Customers come into the bank with a handful of debts from
> department stores, oil companies, finance companies and the
> bank and want to combine this mess into one big loan—
> usually by stretching out the payments. I used to think that
> this was a reasonable solution but I don't any longer. All too
> often, we get these people set up with a consolidation loan, pay
> off their old debts, and figure that they will be better off. Then
> we find out a few months later that they just went out of the
> bank and started all over again borrowing from the same peo-
> ple. Debt consolidation only works if it is backed up by wiser
> use of credit. Otherwise it does more harm than good.

The Overcommitted Debtor

"The money you never knew you had," says the
pamphlet from the Bank of Montreal, backed up by a picture of a smiling woman holding out a wad of twenty-
dollar bills. How would you interpret that phrase? Like almost everybody else, you would think that somewhere
there is money that belongs solely to you, free and unen-
cumbered. Money in a long-lost bank account, an inheritance you did not know about, or gold coins in your back-
yard.

Think again. Open up the pamphlet and you find out
what the Bank of Montreal means.

> Action Money. The uncomplicated loan from the Bank of
> Montreal. Action money is the money you never knew you
> had . . . a loan but better than that. It's low in cost and life
> insured. Chances are all you need to get it is a steady job and

the Bank of Montreal. Because your credit at the Bank of Montreal's just sitting there, waiting to be activated.

If that is not misleading and socially irresponsible advertising, it is time that there was a new definition of acceptable advertising. Only the most twisted thinking could claim that a bank loan is money you never knew you had. It is this very attitude that creates inflationary pressures through an excessive amount of consumer spending and leads to the problem of the overcommitted debtor.

Data on the number of overcommitted debtors in Canada is difficult to come by, but there are indications that excess personal debt is a serious problem. Personal bankruptcies increased 724.5 percent from 1967 to 1977, and consumer credit is now 23 percent of net disposable income. Debt counselling services report a huge increase in the number of their clients, and approximately 25 percent of loans with finance companies are in arrears. Conservative estimates place one out of ten Canadians in the category of the overcommitted debtor.

Overzealous lenders are a large part of this problem, but it is also important to realize that all the blame cannot be placed on the companies who make the loans. The individuals who get themselves into these financial messes are also at fault. Our laws and customs say that every adult who is mentally competent can borrow as much money as he wishes no matter how small or unstable his income is. This places a great deal of responsibility on the consumer. Unfortunately, though, most overcommitted debtors know very little about managing their personal finances.

There is no doubt that the consumer needs to be better educated about credit, starting with late primary and high school courses with programs continuing on through adult life. This is an expensive and long-term solution. But it is not the total answer because it will never give protection to those people who cannot fend for themselves for reasons of health, age, or inexperience.

Ontario passed a law called the Consumer Protection Act which gave the Registrar of the Consumer Protection Bureau the power to move against advertising that is deceptive or misleading. The Consumer Protection Act also requires financial ads to disclose enough information for a consumer to make a reasonable comparison of loan terms. But the act falls short in one aspect of the debt problem, which many people believe is its root. It fails to focus on the whole push for the public to use consumer credit freely and to the maximum amount allowed by the banking system.

From time to time, other ways have been tried to restrict the growth of consumer credit such as increasing the required size of down payments or restricting the terms of loans. These measures were usually part of a general economic policy during a national emergency like World War II or the Korean War. They were not very effective because they could be easily evaded and were difficult or even impossible to apply to such forms of credit as revolving charge accounts at department stores.

The best solution to the problem of the overcommitted debtor is legislation that not only applies specifically to this problem but is also integrated into other legislation covering banking institutions and consumer protection. And the legislation must be backed by government agencies that have the power and funding to be sure that the laws are being obeyed. There is no point in having laws that are on the books but never enforced. It is equally important that the agencies be readily available to the consumer in most urban centres so that they can advise the consumer and come to his aid when help is needed.

The Receivership Racket

Individual consumers do have some protection against unfair practices by banking institutions if they cannot pay their loans, but small businesses have very little. A study by the Vancouver *Sun* in March 1978 showed that many small businesses went bankrupt because of the "incompetence, deceit and broken promises of some of society's most trusted institutions—bankers, lawyers, appraisers, government officials, politicians and court-appointed trustees. In some of the cases the courts themselves have been used as instruments of deceit. In others, the courts and laws governing bankruptcies are being circumvented by the ever-increasing use of receiverships."[8]

At that time, about thirty companies were being put in receivership by the banks in British Columbia each month. This is a simple legal matter to arrange. Any company that does not instantly pay a demand loan can be put into receivership and the receiver can do anything lawful to raise money for the creditor. Any of the assets of the company can be sold for a nickel on the dollar. The receiver can be appointed at the same time the demand loan is called and the owner of the business stripped of all his assets so fast he has no chance to fight. By the time he has caught his breath, called his lawyer, and tried to raise some money, his company may be sold out from under him for almost nothing.

The *Sun* found a case where the Bank of Montreal put a company into receivership over a debenture on which the bank had not loaned out any money. The bank told the court that it had demanded repayment before the debenture was signed.

The *Sun* also stressed the chronic problem faced by the little guy when he is bucking the big financial institutions, or for that matter, faced by the reporter or business writer who wants to get real facts on banking abuses. "When it comes to bank practices," Paul Raugust wrote,

> . . . the people in the know are extremely reluctant to risk the wrath of banks by talking about them in public. The best legal minds and the top accounting firms are retained by the banks for the much sought after and highly profitable receivership and bankruptcy work. Even businessmen who have had problems with banks would rather not talk for fear of jeopardizing existing loans.
>
> Some bankers themselves admit their careers would be over if they talked. Retired bankers could risk their pensions by talking as each one of them is required to swear an oath of secrecy with the bank.[9]

Do Women Have a Great Credit-Ability Gap?

Chatelaine claimed in their August 1975 issue that women have a harder time getting credit than men. Writer Ann Berkeley had plenty of stories to prove it.

—A married woman in Ontario, an advertising executive in her late thirties and head of her household, wanted a house for herself and her children but couldn't get a mortgage without the signature of her 79-year-old pensioner father.

—A divorced woman earning a healthy salary in Montreal was told she couldn't get an American Express card unless her ex-husband cosigned for her.

—A woman earning $20,000 a year was told by Diners Club to get the signature of her husband who earned $7,000 a year less than she did.

—A large department store, says Laura Sabia of the Ontario Status of Women Council, told a widow she could have credit if her 16-year-old son cosigned for her.

—Two relatives of women working for the federal Advisory Council on the Status of Women, one from Toronto, the other from Ottawa, tried to open charge accounts in stores and were refused unless their husbands' names were on the card.

—A regularly employed single woman in her early thirties was unable to get a loan to buy a vacation home, despite having cash for a substantial downpayment. Yet her fiancé, a former bankrupt, easily got a loan to buy the same property with a smaller downpayment.

Nearly every woman who has tried to get credit can tell similar stories, even though there is no doubt that women do not have the same degree of difficulty getting credit that they had five years ago. Today women still meet with some prejudice and ignorance, and the infuriating aspect of the credit situation for women is that they should ever have to fight for an equal access to credit. Some department stores are particularly difficult about granting credit cards to women. Sears still often asks for the husband's signature although they will give a woman a card without the signature if she demands it.

The plight of widows can be equally severe. Many of them have their credit cards cancelled as soon as the credit grantor finds out the husband is dead. Then when she applies for a new one, she is refused.

But take heart. The important thing to remember is that discrimination in most financial institutions is no longer company policy. It is usually something practiced by a few individual loan personnel whose minds are still functioning in a pre-Boer War mode. When a woman encounters this sort of thing she should just walk across the street. There is always a reputable financial institution that will loan money to any borrower who is financially sound.

Single women, in particular, have noticed a great improvement in their access to credit. Fifteen years ago, the

Dean of Women at a large Western Canadian university had to get her brother to cosign her mortgage. At the same time, an unmarried investment analyst in Vancouver was subjected to intense grilling and a sermon on the evils of speculation by single women every time she asked the loan manager at the Commerce for credit to buy blue-chip securities. She wisely moved to the Bank of Montreal where they were very accommodating. It is most unlikely that you would encounter this attitude today. If it occurs, as it still does occasionally, it is not directed solely at single women. Men can also get the same nonsense.

The story is quite different when a woman marries. This is where the crunch comes. Her credit rating goes in with her husband's. It does not matter how financially responsible she is, she will not get credit if her husband has a bad rating. For that reason alone, a woman should always insist that her credit file at credit reporting agencies be kept separately. It also stands her in good stead if she becomes widowed, divorced, or separated. She has established a credit record on her own and it will not be necessary to start from scratch.

Married women also encounter problems when the banks overplay the "protecting the little woman" act. When a successful and married businesswoman wanted to borrow money to buy a car, the bank manager insisted that she obtain a lawyer's permission to take out the loan. This is a ridiculous hangover from the old banking practice of insisting that a wife have a legal opinion before cosigning a business loan for her husband because some wives were so financially naïve or stupid that they might be forced into risky financial situations by their husbands.

The frequent practice of requiring husband and wife to cosign a loan is another problem area, especially since new laws on family relations were passed by provincial governments. Most demands by bank managers for a husband to cosign a wife's loan were just unnecessary and annoying in the past. Marnie Princeton found that out. In 1979 she was in her last year of training for her accounting degree and had a steady job at a good salary. She also owned several revenue-producing properties which carried small mortgages. Marnie asked the manager of her credit union for a loan to buy another property. "OK," he said, "but only if your husband cosigns the loan."

A much more serious problem arises when the banks use a double standard in granting credit. A young woman in Vancouver was asked to cosign a car loan that her husband was taking out. After making six payments, her husband took off for New Brunswick with his girl friend—in the new car. He never made another payment on the loan.

The bank had the option of chasing the husband and trying to seize the car. But that would have been a lot of trouble. Instead, they demanded that the wife make good on the loan. She had a three-year-old son to support and worked as a waitress in a coffee shop. She was barely able to support the two of them and there was no way she could pay off the loan. Fortunately, she went to the provincial government for debt assistance and was advised to declare bankruptcy. She really had no other option. The incredible part of this situation is that based on her own income the woman would have been refused a loan in her own right, but she was held responsible for this large debt.

The cosigning problem becomes more complicated in provinces where new family relations acts give both marriage partners an equal share in the family assets. Under these circumstances, the bank has to take extra precaution to protect itself from loss in case of marriage breakdown.

This could happen if the husband borrowed to buy the family car but the wife received the car as her share of the family assets. The husband is liable for the debt but the bank no longer has a loan secured by an asset. To avoid this situation, banks now require both husband and wife to cosign all loans secured by any asset that could be shared in a marriage settlement.

This wide range of problems that women encounter in credit granting shows that it is not a problem that lends itself to quick or facile remedies. It is just another aspect of the banking scene that the federal government chooses to overlook in its recommendations for changes in banking regulation.

There is a solution, however, through appeal to the Canadian Human Rights Commission. The "Action Line" column in the Vancouver *Province* received a letter from a woman in North Vancouver who was clearly a victim of sex discrimination by a bank. She had been making the payments on her house mortgage for four years during her marriage separation and, now that she was getting a divorce, she wanted the mortgage renewed in her name. The bank insisted that the house be reappraised for a fee of $340 and that her husband cosign the loan.

"Action Line" took the case up with the Canadian Human Rights Commission because, in their words,

> It's a problem we've seen before with other financial institutions and readers should know what to do if this happens to them. We agree with your statement that you should have been accepted or rejected solely on the basis of your ability to pay. And since you have been paying for the past four years without any difficulty, we would have to agree that you seem to have a legitimate complaint against the bank. Federally chartered banks fall within the jurisdiction of the C.H.R.C. because the Human Rights Act specifically prohibits discrimination on the basis of sex and marital status.[10]

"Action Line" advised the woman to write a formal letter of complaint to the CHRC because it looked as though she had a valid complaint. This form of protest against discrimination is only applicable when chartered banks and federally incorporated trust companies are concerned. Other trust companies and credit unions have provincial charters and so come under provincial jurisdiction.

Most financial institutions officially support the principle of no discrimination in credit granting. Abuses generally occur at the branch level and a complaint to the head office is usually effective in resolving the problem.

11

Mortgages

A home of one's own is part of the family dream. It reflects the strong feeling that Canadians have for the land and their need for roots and a space of their own. Only the type of home changes with time. It is no longer the vine-covered cottage with a white picket fence, or even the three-bedroom box in the suburbs. It may now be the condominium or town house in the centre of the city, the suburban rancher, or an older home in the inner city. Whatever form the house takes, the owner probably needs a mortgage to finance the purchase. And this is where the dream can turn into a nightmare or at least a bad headache if it is not financed carefully.

A home is probably the most important investment most people ever make. Nearly half of the typical family's assets are tied up in its home and the mortgage on that home makes up the largest portion of the family debt.

Where do most Canadians get their mortgages? From the banking system. The banks, credit unions, and trust and loan companies provide most of the money for residential mortgages.

Not too long ago, the largest source of money for residential mortgages was the life insurance industry. Trailing well behind were the trust and loan companies. The credit unions did a small part of the business and the banks were inconsequential.

The picture now is entirely different: The life insurance companies prefer commercial and industrial mortgages; the banks are in the market and the credit unions are yapping at their heels; the trust and loan companies are fighting to keep out their competition.

One of the most important participants in the Canadian mortgage market is Canada Mortgage and Housing Corporation, a Crown Corporation of the Federal Government which insures mortgages qualifying under the National Housing Act and provides loan assistance for building homes for low-income families. With NHA mortgages it's possible to borrow up to 95 percent of the purchase price (or appraised value of the house, if it is less) compared to 80 percent for the usual conventional loan. The funds for the mortgages are provided by private lenders such as the banks and trust companies, but these lenders are protected against loss by the insurance provided by CMHC.

In general, the consumer has fared well in this more competitive mortgage market. The banks have forced mortgage rates down, especially in smaller communities where the only financial institution is a small bank branch. There is a fair amount of truth in the statement made before the Bank Act Revisions Committee by Robert M. MacIntosh, chairman of the Canadian Bankers' Association, that most of the briefs presented to the committee lamenting competition from the banks "have been notably lacking in reference to the public interest. To limit the role of the banks, as proposed by the trust and loan companies, amounts to saying that the housebuyer should pay a higher rate of interest for his mortgage loan."[1]

Rates are not the only area in which increased competition has been beneficial to the consumer. The whole subject of prepayment has finally been opened up to real competition. The system that was applied to nearly all mortgages until a few years ago was that no mortgage could be prepaid before five years, and after that only a fixed percentage, usually carrying a penalty of three months' interest on the amount prepaid. The government originally proposed to reduce the lock-in to three years or to eliminate penalties for prepayment of mortgage loans, but this met with a great deal of opposition from the banking institutions. It would create problems for them in balancing the term of the money they borrow with the term of the money they lend. There is also the question of the fairness of borrowers having the option of paying off their loan at any time when lenders cannot collect the loan freely.

Although the proposal died with the Borrowers' and Depositors' Protection Act, the consumer does have more choice now. Today, terms on mortgages run from one to five years and there are several prepayment options. Most financial institutions offer consumers a choice between a closed mortgage—with a fixed term and three months' to six months' interest penalty if the loan is repaid early—or an open mortgage—with prepayment options.

When considering these different options, a consumer must also be sure to really understand the meaning of the word "term." A mortgage term is the length of time during which your interest rate is fixed. Most mortgages now have a term of one to five years. At the end of the term, the interest rate must be renegotiated for another term.

A significant point to realize about a mortgage term is the fact that the principal of the mortgage loan has not necessarily been repaid at the end of the mortgage term.

When you take out a mortgage loan, you will find that the mortgage lender assumes that you will not pay off the loan for twenty-five years if it is a conventioned loan or maybe forty years if it is an NHA mortgage. This extended period of time is called the amortization period. Nearly all mortgages used to have a set rate of interest for the whole amortization period. In those cases the term of the mortgage is the same as the amortization period. A conventional mortgage had a twenty-five year amortization period during which the interest rate was fixed and the monthly payments were the same.

Some financial institutions got into hot water on this type of lending when the interest rates began shooting up. They had loaned money out at 7 percent while they were being forced to borrow money at 9 percent. That was obviously a losing proposition. Now with much shorter terms, it is easier for the financial institutions to match the cost of their assets with the cost of their liabilities.

For the consumer, the advantages are less obvious. You now have a $60,000 mortgage at 10 percent interest requiring monthly payments of $537. The term is up and you have to renegotiate the loan at current interest rates of 15 percent. Now the monthly payment is $748, an increase of 39 percent.

What to Look for When You Are Shopping for a Mortgage

Find out what the interest rate really is and be sure that you are comparing equals. A difference of ¼ of 1 percent on a 25-year mortgage of $50,000 adds up to an extra cost of $2,600.

Financial institutions calculate interest in several ways.

Some calculate it semiannually while others do it monthly, and that can make quite a difference. Federal laws say that the interest rate on a mortgage must be stated on an annual basis, calculated semiannually, not in advance. But that is not always the way it is advertised.

Credit unions in particular have misled many mortgage buyers this way. The credit union would advertise that it had mortgage money available at 13.75 percent. Most mortgage buyers accept this at its face value. Only a few of them really read the mortgage document which was required by law to disclose that the rate was really 14.15 percent. The low rate was a monthly calculation, but the true rate and the higher one was the legally-required semiannual rate.

Interest is not the only cost in taking out a mortgage. There are others, so be sure that you get them in writing in advance; it can make quite a difference. Be aware that some mortgage lenders charge a bonus or a commission and there are legal fees and appraisal fees.

Legal fees are usually ½ of 1 percent of the amount of the mortgage. There are also other disbursements such as land registry fees. Appraisal fees usually run between $100 and $300. But be warned that you might have to pay an appraisal fee even if you do not get the mortgage. What is even worse, you may not get to keep the appraisal even though you pay for it. The bank will insist on keeping it— for no significant reason and even though it is not entitled to do so.

An investment dealer asked a western bank for a home improvement loan. He and his bank manager agreed on the amount of the loan and the interest rate that should be charged on it, subject only to an appraisal confirming that the house had a value at least as high as its owner had estimated. He was asked to authorize an appraisal, which he did. He was then told it would have to be submitted to the head office for approval.

When the report came back to the branch level, the investment dealer learned that the appraisal placed a value on the house even higher than he had estimated. Nevertheless the head office of the bank insisted on a rate 1 percent higher than had been agreed upon earlier. They also wanted $125 for the appraisal, but they would not let the house owner have the document. He paid the $125 but he went elsewhere for this mortgage.

Legally, the home-owner could have sued the bank in Small Debts Court to get his appraisal, but he did not know this.

Most mortgages have a fixed rate of interest for a definite period. One should select a term based on the expected trend of interest rates, although few people can predict rates accurately. If interest rates are expected to go up, the bank will want its customer to take out a one-year-term mortgage because they can charge more when it is renewed in the following year. If interest rates are in a downtrend, the consumer will want a one-year mortgage because he can refinance it next year at a lower rate.

A survey by Metropolitan Trust showed that older and more affluent householders preferred short-term mortgages with flexible interest rates to the regular five-year variety. While some of these people may be betting on interest rates, the more likely explanation is that they plan to repay the mortgage early.

Mortgage borrowers like to have the option of repaying part or all of their mortgage early without a penalty. By law, this can be done any time after five years, provided it includes a three-month interest penalty. National Housing Act mortgages have some special provisions allowing prepayment of up to 10 percent of the original amount of the loan with the twelfth monthly payment and the twenty-fourth monthly payment. Any part of the outstanding balance can be prepaid once a year after three years. All prepayments require a three-month interest penalty.

Open mortgages are a current fashion among some mortgage lenders. They allow the borrower to make either partial or total prepayment of the mortgage. This could be a big advantage for the borrower because the interest is calculated on the outstanding balance of the loan. The lower the principal amount of the loan, the lower the interest costs will be over the whole life of the mortgage.

But there is always a catch. In this case, it is a higher rate of interest. Many mortgage lenders charge ¼ of 1 percent over their regular mortgage rate for an open payment privilege. Each person must decide if this cost is worth it through a complicated calculation involving one's tax bracket, investment plans, and estimated income. It may be too expensive, or it might just boil down to relief at getting the mortgage out of the way.

The change to short-term mortgages with a long amortization period leads to the problem of what you do when the mortgage must be renewed. A mortgage with a five-year term must be renewed at the end of the five years or you have to pay off the balance that is still outstanding. So when you go to your previously friendly banker to negotiate for the next five years, you may find that he prefers to finance spaghetti factories instead of making mortgage loans, or maybe his interest rate has gone up by 4 percent. The mortgage lender is not obligated to renew the loan unless he has specifically agreed in advance to do so.

Some banking institutions do guarantee that they will renew the mortgage throughout the entire amortization period if the borrower has made payments regularly. This is the type of lender to deal with, but get it in writing.

Mortgage borrowers also need to scrutinize insurance charges carefully. They can be faced with three possible types of insurance costs—mortgage insurance, life insurance, and disability insurance. The borrower may choose to take out disability insurance enabling him to continue his mortgage payments when he would otherwise be unable to because of illness or injuries. One may take out life insurance to pay off a mortgage in the event of death. The rates vary between different financial institutions, so they should be checked out carefully.

The banks claim that the sale of insurance is not designed to make money for them. In one of their booklets prepared for the Bank Act revision they came out with this strange statement.

> It should be pointed out that this procedure (selling life insurance to cover the outstanding liability under mortgages) is not one that gives the banks any direct return, or if it does, it is a very minor one. Furthermore, the borrower enters into a contract with an insurance company which has undertaken to provide this service, not with the bank. The main objective of the bank is to offer a convenience to its customers.[2]

Mortgage insurance is a different matter. It is a requirement on certain types of mortgage loans to protect the lender. It is paid by the borrower. National Housing Act mortgages require insurance as do conventional mortgages where the amount of the mortgage is a high percentage of the appraised value of the property. It varies between 7/8 of a percent to 1¼ percent of the amount of the mortgage. While these requirements appear to place an added burden on the consumer, it should be realized that the lender would probably refuse to make the loan without them. Mortgage insurance is a reasonable requirement on a loan where the borrower makes a small down payment. Fire insurance is also essential.

One area where there is absolutely no doubt that consumers are being ripped off is that of property taxes. All mortgages made by banking institutions require the property owner to make monthly payments of his property taxes. This money is accumulated in a special property tax account during the year and then, when the taxes are due to the municipality, the money is paid out. A pamphlet called *All About TD Mortgages,* put out by the Toronto-Dominion Bank, describes its special property tax account, then says, "This convenience to you is arranged at no extra cost." That statement should qualify for the Ludicrous Statement of The Year Award. The fact is that this account differs very little from a savings account on which interest is paid on at least the minimum monthly balance at a relatively high rate. In a tax account you get 3 percent interest.

The Inspector General of Banks has had complaints about this but so far has done nothing about it. An official of a chartered bank said nothing had been done about it because so few people had complained. Clearly that is the way it will stay until enough people do complain.

Mortgage borrowers can also run into problems over the qualifying income of the spouse, most often the female spouse. Until recently banking institutions put a low value on the income of wives when considering borrowers' ability to repay their mortgages. The standard sort of formula is to add up the male wage-earner's salary or wages, his investment or other income, and some percentage of the female spouse's income. The Canadian Imperial Bank of Commerce, for example, says in a pamphlet called *Mortgage Loans,* "You may be able to include the income of your spouse to qualify for a mortgage loan but the amount of such earnings which will be considered varies with each case." Like with whether she is on the pill or has been sterilized. Many women report that they were asked embarrassing questions like that by mortgage lenders. Do you suppose they ever ask about vasectomies?

Other banks are more enlightened, although they are very cagey about the exact amount of a spouse's income they will include. The Bank of Montreal says that up to 100 percent of a spouse's income may be used in income estimates. The TD just leaves the impression that all the spouse's income is included, although in their pamphlet *All About TD Mortgages* her income is 54 percent of his.

The New Mortgage World—An Alphabet Soup of GPMs, RAMs, and VRMs

Ordinary mortgages may be going the way of the dodo. Not only are there open mortgages instead of closed mortgages, there are also Graduated Payment Mortgages (sometimes called Flexible Loan Insurance Programs), Reverse Annuity Mortgages (sometimes called Independent Income Mortgages), and Variable Rate Mortgages. If one thought it was difficult to decide between relatively simple types of mortgages, these far more complicated ones will be really baffling. But they are worth looking at because they do have advantages for some people.

The GPM

Graduated Payment Mortgages were dreamed up as an antidote to the growing problem of the young family without sufficient current income to buy the house they would like to own. If the family's income rises over the years and even if house prices increase, the family will be able to make bigger mortgage payments in the future. Ergo—why not have mortgages which have a low monthly payment in the first year but a gradually increasing one over the next ten years and constant payments for the balance of the mortgage? Enter the GPM.

The trouble with this plan is that family income may not increase sufficiently to make the higher payments, and house prices may hold at current levels or even fall. In this case the house will be overmortgaged, for it may take fifteen years for the principal of the mortgage to get back down to its original amount. For example, with a $40,000, 30-year mortgage at 11 percent, payments during the early years do not even cover the total interest cost, let alone the principal. The result is that the amount of the mortgage actually increases for a number of years until the payments rise to the point when they cover the full principal payment as well as some of the interest costs. In this example, the principal amount of the $40,000 mortgage keeps rising until it is $44,143 in the ninth year; then it gradually falls until it is back to $40,000 in the fifteenth year. Thus the home-owner is paying considerably more interest through the life of the mortgage than he would if he took out a conventional mortgage with constant monthly payments.

If the mortgage lender demands that the yearly mortgage payments cannot be greater than 25 percent of the borrower's annual income, a conventional mortgage for $40,000 would require an annual mortgage income of $20,000, but a GPM would require an annual income of only $15,000. The GPM would then allow the householder with the lower income to buy a bigger house.

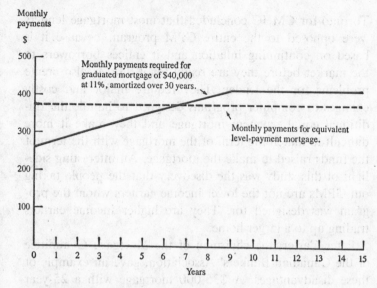

Monthly payments $

Monthly payments required for graduated mortgage of $40,000 at 11%, amortized over 30 years.

Monthly payments for equivalent level-payment mortgage.

Years

Source: *The Financial Post*, October 21, 1978.

Canada Mortgage and Housing Corporation proposed a GPM program in the spring of 1978 to replace the widely criticized Assisted Home Ownership Program (AHOP) which had a default rate of 8 percent. By overencouraging building developers and marginal home buyers, the program left some communities plugged up with foreclosed or unsold AHOP homes. The same result is predicted by many observers for the GPM program.

Many banking institutions have refused to participate in it. Of the thirteen mortgage lenders surveyed, only two banks and three trust companies have done any GPM lending. The others believe GPMs are financially unsound and that they create problems for the lender. In the United States they are often called "Gyp Ems."

A survey conducted by Clayton Research Associates of

Toronto for CMHC concluded that most mortgage lenders were opposed to the entire GPM program because it is based on continuing inflation and it entices borrowers to the market before they are ready for it. GPMs also create problems for the lender. They require major and costly changes to computer programs designed to handle the traditional equal payment mortgage and they make it more difficult to match the term of the mortgage with the term of the funds raised to make the mortgage. An interesting sidelight of this study was the discovery that the people taking out GPMs are not the lower income earners whom the program was designed for. They are higher income earners trading up to a larger home.

Peter Carter, the chairman of the Mortgage Committee of the Canadian Bankers' Association, gave an example of these disadvantages. A $35,000 mortgage with a 25-year amortization period and a constant interest rate of 10¼ percent for the entire period would cost the borrower $9,320 less than a GPM. In addition, the original debt of $35,000 in a GPM would increase to $37,000 by the end of 6 years even though the borrower had made mortgage payments of about $20,000. It would take 10 years to bring the principal below the original $35,000 amount.

If house prices do not rise during this time, the mortgage becomes an increasingly large percentage of the value of the house and there could come a time when the house owner decides to pack it up and walk away from the debt burden. He figures his small equity in the house is not worth the continual effort to make the higher and higher mortgage payments, especially if taxes and the cost of maintenance keep going up at the same time. The lender then has to foreclose and go through the cost and bother of liquidating the property.

Vancouver-based First City Financial Corporation

agrees that GPMs are not for everyone, yet they are encouraging many people to take them out. The company reported that it had sold 2,000 GPMs worth about $100 million in the first year they were offered. First City Vice-President Robert Graham says his company is a leader in GPMs in Canada. He thinks, "they are an effort to take into account the desire to buy houses, and the difficulty of it." First City believes that their plan will add new customers and assist marginal buyers to get larger houses. "Some people say Canadians should be like Europeans and lower their expectations, but we don't agree. If a person wants a house, why, in a country as rich as Canada, can't he get a house?"[3]

Even closer to the bone was the comment of Richard M. Griffith, a vice-president of Victoria Wood Development Corporation, about their FLIP (Flexible Loan Insurance Program). "FLIP," according to Griffith, "is a graduated payment mortgage that will allow thousands of Canadian families and individuals to purchase that first or second home now, rather than waiting until they can afford it."[4]

That sort of reasoning sounds suspiciously like the one used to push "red convertible loans." The desire to buy a house is a legitimate aspiration and there are good grounds for believing that home ownership improves social stability and the quality of family life. A very questionable point is the rising expectation of home-owners for elaborate built-ins, utilities, and wall-to-wall carpeting which inflate the cost of housing and lead to the overcommitted debtor.

The federal government appears to be encouraging this kind of overborrowing by consumers because its housing and mortgage lending agency, Canada Mortgage and Housing Corporation, is offering a GPM that appears to be particularly open to abuse. CMHC insures National Housing Act mortgages made by approved lenders such as banks, trust companies, and credit unions. These mortgages are designed to make it easier for lower income earners to buy houses by requiring a down payment of only 5 percent compared to 25 percent on conventional first mortgages. These features of regular NHA mortgages were favourable enough in times of lower interest rates, but the much higher rates of 1979 and 1980 made it impossible for many people to meet the payments on even an NHA mortgage. Consequently CMHC proposed a new scheme requiring only a 5 percent down payment and initial monthly payments that are only 75 percent of the payments on a regular NHA mortgage. The trouble with this idea is that the mortgage borrower can end up owing more money than the house is worth within a few years, because the interest payments are so large.

What is there to deter the home-owner from walking away from this debt load?

Even private lenders try to avoid this kind of risk by stipulating that the size of the mortgage debt can never exceed the original purchase price. And the down payment must be at least 14 percent of the purchase price if the mortgage payments in the first year are only 75 percent of conventional mortgage payments.

The mortgage lenders like banks and trust companies that also normally make NHA mortgages did not like the risk they foresaw in this CMHC graduated payment mortgage and they were reluctant to make these mortgages. To get the business, CMHC decided to offer them a sweetener. It will take over the mortgages if arrears exceed three months. The implication of this is that CMHC (i.e., the taxpayer) will absorb the entire risk of overlending. As *The Financial Post* commented, "So there are no longer any checks or balances, no rules for circumspection. The borrower can borrow with hardly any money down. The lender can lend with scant attention to risk. And CMHC can subsidize with magnanimous indifference."[5]

Some savings and loan institutions in the United States and credit unions in Western Canada do support the GPMs, however, and Quebec credit unions also encourage them. It will take five or six years of experience with GPMs to know who is right; in the meantime, the consumer should look at GPMs with considerable skepticism.

RAMs

Reverse Annuity Mortgages can also present pitfalls. Take the case of an elderly widow who has lived in the same small house for thirty-five years. She is proud of her garden and her home and manages to look after most of it herself. But taxes and the upkeep of the house are rising all the time and at a faster rate than her small pension. She could sell the house and move into an apartment, but tending her house and garden are what keep the old lady going. Is there a way to let her stay in her house and keep up with the costs of home ownership?

There is, although at a cost. She could put a Reverse Annuity Mortgage on her home; then the mortgage company would pay her a regular monthly annuity. The clue here is the word "annuity," which means a regular return of capital plus interest if you are the lender, or minus interest if you are the borrower. The home-owner with a RAM is a borrower who is consuming the capital in his home at a certain interest cost.

This is the opposite of the usual mortgage situation. With each payment of a RAM, the mortgage increases until at some time the whole mortgage debt must be repaid. In addition, the home-owner pays interest on the mortgage which adds more to the debt. This can all add up in ten years to a large sum and a large percentage of the value of the house.

If the value of the house has climbed during the life of the RAM, there may still be a fair amount of equity left. This is what the home-owner is gambling on if the house must be sold to pay the debt. Very few home-owners who take out a RAM are going to have the money to pay off the mortgage debt from their savings. They will have to sell their home to do so.

Some elderly home-owners will undoubtedly die before the RAM matures, in which case there is no problem except for heirs who may not like seeing their inheritance whittled down. For those who live long enough, there could be a serious financial situation if housing prices do not rise enough to leave them with some capital. Promotional material for RAMs does not usually mention this possibility. Instead it dwells on the past record of rising housing prices.

Metro Trust introduced a RAM called the Independent Income Mortgage (IIM). It is a first mortgage designed to provide an income flow for ten years through a series of renewable one-year mortgages. The lender and the borrower decide how much income the home-owner wants annually. If it is appropriate to the value of the house, the lender figures out the annual size of the mortgage that will provide interest to the lender and income to the borrower. The interest is deducted by the lender and the borrower receives the balance of the mortgage payment.

An example given by William Hunt, vice-president for the western region of Metro Trust, is that of an older couple who own an $80,000 house. They want additional income of $3,000 each year. If they take out an 11 percent IIM, they would receive $30,000 over the ten years and accumulate a $59,100 mortgage.

If the property rises in value during this time at an average rate of 3½ percent (which is well below the rate of the last ten years), the house will be worth $112,800 or $32,800 more at the end of the ten years. Hunt says, "Using these figures, the IIM would show no cost at all. The gain would actually be $4,000, assuming the house was sold for its new higher value in 10 years."[6] The $30,000 income and the $32,800 capital gain in the house has exceeded the mortgage of $59,100 by $3,700.

Proponents of RAMs believe there are major social advantages in providing an income flow to older people on fixed incomes. Allowing senior citizens to stay in their homes for a longer time reduces the pressure on publicly financed senior citizens' housing. But it will only do this in the long run if property values keep going up or homeowners with RAMs die before the mortgage is due and payable. If property values do not rise enough and the home-owner lives a long time, he or she will be left with much less to live on and be far more likely to require financial assistance from the government. In other words, RAMs are a speculation on inflation and mortality.

VRMs

Variable Rate Mortgages are another new type of mortgage. Mortgage lenders do not like making mortgages for long periods of time at fixed interest rates if they think rates are going up. That is why they thought up the idea of VRMs. These are mortgages that allow the lender to adjust the interest rate on a mortgage up or down depending on some index of the cost of money.

The chart of mortgage interest rates shows how rates have fluctuated over the past nine years. The interest rate on a VRM mortgage would have risen from 1972 to 1974, fallen in 1973 briefly, and then risen again. There would have been another drop in rates in 1976, a steady period, and then a sharp rise in 1978 which would extend through 1980. Clearly the whole period favoured the lender of VRMs more than it did the borrower of VRMs.

After VRMs were introduced in California in 1975 by some savings and loan companies, two of the largest of these made 80 percent of all their new mortgage loans in the form of VRMs. This was great for the savings and loan associations because they were insulating themselves from the usual money squeeze that banking institutions feel when rates rise. In 1979, the cost of their money (savings accounts, term deposits, etc.) was almost as high as the rate on conventional mortgages so there was very little profit to be made from that kind of mortgage lending. VRMs saved the day. But it is questionable if consumers benefit in the long run.

Initially they may benefit because VRMs allow the consumer to buy a bigger house or get mortgage money more easily. Some lenders also offer the inducement of a slightly lower initial interest rate and the right to transfer the mortgage at its current rate if the house is sold. It is also a fact that interest rates can go down but the history of the past ten years offers scant hope of this occurring for any significant period of time.

Mortgage Interest Rates

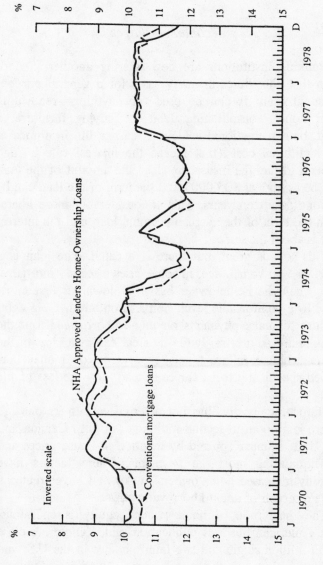

Source: *Canadian Housing Statistics 1973, Central Mortgage and Housing Corporation, Statistics Canada: Financial Institutions*

Second Mortgages

Banking institutions are now offering another kind of loan that substitutes in many cases for a general purpose personal loan. It can be used for anything—renovating your home, consolidating debts, or buying furniture, a boat, or a recreational vehicle. It carries life insurance at no additional cost (that means the interest rate is high enough to pay the insurance, since the amount of the loan can be as high as $35,000) and the term of the loan can be as long as fifteen years. This is considerably more liberal than the term of the average personal loan and the interest rate is about the same.

This sounds great, but there is a catch. The loan is a mortgage on your home, in some cases a second mortgage. Just when the home-owner has paid down his first mortgage to a comfortable level, he tacks on another big debt. Failure to make payments on money borrowed from the bank and used arbitrarily to buy a car can mean loss of the home, whereas failure to make payments on money borrowed specifically for a car can mean only the loss of the car.

Unfortunately, this has not deterred consumers one bit. There is a boom in second mortgages in both Canada and the United States, spurred by inflation in house prices and self-liquidating mortgage payments. These factors have steadily increased home-owners' equity and have created a huge reservoir of unused borrowing power.

The magnitude of home-owners' equity is enormous. One American business publication said, "There are close to 55 million single and two-family homes in the U.S. and their combined worth must be near $2 trillion. Subtract from that over $500 billion in mortgage debt and the American homeowner is left with a home ownership equity of $1.5 trillion."[7]

Once again, the consumer and the banking system are using inflation to fuel a higher and higher level of consumer debt—where does the buck stop?

12

Bank Credit Cards

The most revolutionary slogan in common use today is not one dreamed up by a radical political group. It is an advertising slogan concocted by the banks, that very catchy question, "Will that be cash or Visa?"

Widespread use of credit cards is the beginning of a shift in the whole way that our economy functions. Early in history, we used cash, then we began using cheques, until the system got choked up with the huge volume of paper. Enter the bank credit card with all its advantages in the new computer world. And we see it persistently supplanting cash and cheques. Credit cards provide an automatic line of credit, are widely accepted by merchants, and let the user avoid the disadvantages of carrying too much cash. They are easy to use, often too easy to use, and this can lead to one of their disadvantages. The banks have also built some features into the credit card system which are not to the advantage of the consumer.

Taking a longer range viewpoint, the consumer should be even more concerned about the role of credit cards in

the gradual shift of our economic life from a card-based society to the cashless society, or more correctly the less-cash
society when almost all financial transactions will be fun-
nelled through the computers of the electronic funds
transfer system.

For the banking system, there are obvious advantages in
persuading consumers to shift to credit cards. To begin
with, it cuts down on the enormous volume of paperwork
in a society addicted to writing cheques. Each cheque is
handled about fourteen times as it is processed in the banking system, and there are ten million cheques to process
each day. Secondly, bank credit cards provide a larger volume of consumer credit paying higher interest rates at a
lower cost to the banking system.

It is no wonder that bank credit cards are being pro-
moted heavily. Chargex and Master Charge spent over $4
million on advertising in 1977.[1] The banks are also ingenious at dreaming up new services that are available only to
card holders. It is not possible to get a Commerce Key Account or Royal Certified Service without having a Visa
card. The new country-wide chequing service offered by
the Bank of Montreal requires a MasterCard card, and
cash dispensing machines like the Montreal's Instabank
require a special MasterCard card.

This drive by the banking system to get consumers con-
ditioned to using their credit cards many times a month for
many different uses has been enormously successful. The
use of bank credit cards has been rising at a rate of 25 to
30 percent a year. Before long, consumers will be able to
use their cards for all their shopping, utility bills, and tax
payments through instantaneous deductions from their
chequing account or automatic overdrafts and lines of
credit.

By this time, everyone will have his own universal bank

TYPES OF CREDIT CARDS

Types	Issued By
BANK CREDIT CARDS	
Visa	Canadian Imperial Bank of Commerce, Royal Bank, Bank of Nova Scotia, Toronto-Dominion Bank, affiliated with Bank of America and Barclay Bank
MasterCard	Bank of Montreal, National Bank of Canada, affiliated with many U.S. banks led by Citibank
PRIVATE LABEL CARDS	
Oil Company Cards	Imperial Oil, Gulf, Texaco, Husky, etc.
DEPARTMENT STORE CARDS	Sears, Eaton's, Woodward's, The Bay
TRAVEL AND ENTERTAINMENT CARDS	
American Express	American Express
Diners Club	Diners Club

credit card which will serve as an identification card as well. It will have some almost foolproof method, such as a thumbprint, to restrict its use to one individual; each person with this card will then be a full-fledged participant in the economy. Anyone without it will be an economic outcast of a society that could be more frightening than *1984* unless consumers start planning for it now.

What Bank Credit Cards Have That Other Credit Cards Don't Have

Bank credit cards are like other credit cards in some ways but all their features, taken as a package, make them the most useful, the most economical, and the most convenient—provided people use them properly. The different types of cards are compared on the next page. Note that

Qualifications Needed	Cost	Use
good credit rating	free	buy wide range of goods and services in Canada and abroad, get cash advances
good credit rating	free	buy wide range of goods and services in Canada and abroad, get cash advances
good credit rating	free	oil, gas, tires, batteries, minor repairs, motels
good credit rating	free	usually good only in issuer's stores
higher credit rating, business income of $12,500 or acceptable level of other income	$20 a year	restaurants, hotels, some stores, airlines, car rentals, travellers cheques, cash advances
excellent credit rating, income of at least $12,000	$20 a year	restaurants, car rentals, hotels

bank credit cards are free, relatively easy to obtain, and can be used almost anywhere in the world to buy a wide variety of goods and services and to get cash. Department store cards are free but in most cases they can be used only at stores belonging to one company. Oil company cards are also free but, like store cards, their use is restricted to certain companies and services. Travel and entertainment cards cost $20 a year, have higher credit requirements, and a more restricted list of merchants.

The Credit Card Application

A consumer applying for a credit card must provide the card system with the usual information required on all credit applications, then sign a statement allowing the bank to acquire credit information about him. That part is quite routine. What is not routine is the requirement that the applicant agrees to accept the terms of a cardholder agreement even though he may never have seen one. This is a serious omission. Every application form should be required to include the terms of the agreement because they have some surprising features. Everyone applying for a credit card should ask for the agreement and read it thoroughly.

The banks have very carefully stacked the deck in their favour as careful reading of an agrèement will show. The agreement states that: (1) the cards are the property of the bank; (2) the cardholder's credit privileges can be withdrawn at any time and he must surrender the card when asked by the bank; (3) failure to agree to the terms of the agreement allows the bank to make all card debts immediately payable without giving the cardholder any notice; (4) joint holders of cards are equally liable for any debts incurred with the card; and (5) cardholders must pay the card company for all debts, including any that may have been recorded in error, even if the goods or services are unsatisfactory, a credit voucher was not recorded, or an unauthorized person charged up to $50 on the account before the bank was notified.

The Law Reform Commission does not think much of these cardholder agreements.

> It is sometimes stated that the extreme rigour of the terms found in bank credit card agreements is directed solely to the difficulty of proving fraud in these situations. The broad legal powers taken by the banks are directed, it is said, to making themselves the sole judge of whether such abuses exist—if they do not, the banks settle. If true, such a position is still untenable. The grant of unreviewed legal discretion to a private corporation dealing on manifestly unfair terms cannot be defended. Nor has it ever been demonstrated that the banks have

taken no more power than is necessary to protect their interests.[2]

This is just one of the many aspects of bank credit cards that need revision to give some semblance of a balance of power between consumers and the banking system.

The cardholder should also realize that in law, he has accepted these terms once he uses his card. The use of a credit card is legally covered by the law of contract, and this means that he is confirming the fact that he fully accepts the terms of the cardholder agreement as soon as he uses the card.

The Cardholder's Credit Limit

Each cardholder is assigned a credit limit which establishes the amount of money which he is allowed to charge on his card at any one time. The amount is basically related to his income. The minimum is about $400 with MasterCard and $300 with Visa. The maximum is $3,000, although higher amounts can be negotiated. These limits are not as restrictive as they may initially appear. It is easy in practice to exceed them as long as the cardholder makes minimum monthly payments on time.

Cardholders often wonder why this credit limit keeps going up when they have not requested an increase and their financial position has not changed. A spokesman at the Bank of Montreal said they were reviewed periodically and, if the customers made payments on time, the credit limit was raised. For many consumers, these unsolicited increases in credit limits are due most likely to increased use of their credit cards. The more they buy, the more they can buy. A dangerous and unnecessary practice.

The Monthly Statement

Cardholders receive a statement each month showing a descriptive billing of all their transactions. Errors must be reported within fifteen days, a fact that many people are unaware of. If the consumer does not report the error within that time period, he has no recourse. This situation is just another example of the way in which the banks have weighted the balance of power in their favour, since cardholders could be on holiday or ill or the statement could be held up in the mail or not even delivered.

The Right of Set-off

Do you know what can happen if you don't make a payment on your MasterCard Account? The Bank of Montreal can and will take the money out of your chequing or savings account. This is known as the right of set-off.

Owe money to a bank and it has the right to seize any money in your accounts with that bank. Customers find it particularly amazing when credit card debts from Visa or MasterCard are offset by bank accounts, not realizing that the credit card companies are owned by the banks.

A credit card customer in Ottawa got into financial trouble because he foolishly thought that the bank would cut him off at his $300 credit limit. As big spenders know only too well, it is quite easy to spend well beyond your credit limit if you move quickly and spread it around. In no time at all, this particular credit cardholder had spent twice his limit and run up a debt of $600.

The bank naturally expected higher monthly payments

on this debt and, when the customer could not make them, exercised its legal power under the Bank Act to extract all the money in the customer's bank account. The customer was incensed because he had counted on the credit card company to do his bookkeeping and control his spending.[3]

If there is one lesson to be learned by bank cardholders, this is it. The banks are not your nursemaids. It is up to you to know when you are approaching your credit limitations and, in dire circumstances when it is exceeded, to pull your cash out of any bank connected with your credit card.

The Convenience of a Credit Card

Used properly, a credit card can be a useful and economic tool for consumers who follow a few simple rules. But those consumers who do not follow these rules can easily get into serious trouble with an overload of debt, a ruined credit rating, and large legal expenses. New and greatly improved consumer safeguards are essential, but since these are currently nowhere in sight, consumers must become educated in the wise use of credit cards because everyone will soon *have* to use them. In many cases there will be no choice between cash or Visa and, used sensibly, cards can be very convenient at times.

With a credit card, large purchases can be made without carrying cash, or trying to cash a cheque, or establishing credit with a particular merchant. This is a sensible use of a credit card. All merchants accepting a particular credit card will allow a purchase up to a predetermined floor limit, usually $50, without question, provided the card is not on the master list of lost or stolen cards. Above the floor limit, the merchant must check with the authorization centre to see if the amount of the purchase is within the credit limit assigned to a particular cardholder. If it is, the merchant writes an authorization number on the credit card slip in a specifically designated space labelled "AUTH. NO." The sale is thus completed; a quick and easy process.

A cardholder may now have over two months of free credit before actually having to make a payment on the purchase. A purchase made on the first day of the billing month may not be payable for over 68 days. One sample MasterCard statement, for example, recorded purchases from January 12 to March 22 and carried a statement date of March 22 and a payment date of April 17, a period of 96 days. No matter how long the billing period, however, some payment must be made within 25 days of the statement date.

Credit cards can also function as a form of revolving credit. In this case, consumers can use their cards to buy on time and spread their payments over a longer period. This revolving or open end type of credit means that consumers can continue to make purchases within certain limits as they pay off their old purchases. Unfortunately, this can become a dangerous habit and bears careful watching.

A credit card can also be used to cash a cheque up to a maximum of $500 a day at a participating bank other than the one where the cardholder normally banks. There is no extra charge for this service. Some banks also have cash-dispensing machines which can be activated by special bank credit cards to allow cardholders to withdraw cash from their chequing account without standing in line-ups at a teller's wicket or to get money after banking hours.

A cardholder can get a cash advance for any amount up to the unused portion of his credit limit. In this particular form of credit, the cardholder pays interest on the debt on the first day of the cash advance. There is no free period of credit with cash advances.

Bank credit cards are accepted at banks, stores, hotels, and restaurants in most countries. The amount of purchases or cash obtained outside the country is converted into Canadian dollars before it is recorded on the monthly statement. The time span between the purchase date and the billing date may be much longer than is the case with domestic billings, and this means added free credit for the cardholder.

Pitfalls in Payments

Consumers who use cards these ways must be very careful about their payments. Payments should be made within twenty-five days of the statement date by mailing a cheque or paying in person at any branch of a participating bank. Be sure of the amount of the payment. It is not always clear because the statement often appears to focus attention on the minimum amount owed rather than on the total amount owed.

The amount of the payment can be either the full amount of the bill or a partial payment. It cannot be stressed too often that consumers should be encouraged to pay in full. *Consumer Reports* stated that two-thirds of Americans fail to pay their bills in full on the due date,[4] and in Canada studies show an almost identical record.[5] These unpaid billings on bank credit cards become very profitable loans on the books of the banks.

The partial payment must be at least as large as the minimum amount shown on the statement. A balance of $10 or under must be paid in full. A balance of over $10 will require a minimum payment of at least $10. A balance of over $200 will require a minimum payment equal to 5 percent of the balance.

This partial payment is used, first of all, to pay off any outstanding interest charges; then it is used to pay off any cash advances; and finally it is used to pay off purchases. This method of repayment may result in the cardholder reducing the balance of his principal outstanding very slowly if only the minimum payment is made on a large account. As a consequence, he may never get out of debt. These accounts take on the characteristics of revolving credit. New purchases are continually made as old ones are paid; the consumer is caught in the revolving door of never-ending indebtedness.

Late payments are penalized with a heavy interest charge of 21 percent figured from the date of the last monthly statement, not from the due date of the statement.

The Cost of Buying on Time with a Credit Card

Companies issuing credit cards have a variety of methods for calculating their interest charges, and this can have quite an impact on the actual interest payment. Consumers should pay particular attention to the date on which interest payments start.

A cash advance on a credit card is charged interest from the day the advance is taken while a purchase made on a credit card may not be charged interest for nearly a month. When the interest on a purchase debt is calculated, the department stores generally operate on the closing balance method while the bank credit cards use an average daily balance method.

Woodward's stores, for example, take the closing balance in the charge account at the end of the month and deduct any payments or credit refunds added to the account during the following month to determine the balance on which they will charge interest. A customer owes $450 on November 30 and this becomes the opening balance on December 1. During December she pays $45 into the account. Her adjusted opening balance is now $450 less $45, or $405. Her interest cost for the month of December will be $405 times the interest rate of 1.7 percent per month, or $6.89. Any purchase made during December will not be subject to an interest charge until January.

The bank credit card companies use a different method based on the average daily balance in the account. The finance charge is calculated by adding the balances outstanding on the account on each day of the billing period and then dividing this sum by the number of days in the billing period.

With this method of calculating finance charges, customers should pay their bills as early in the month as possible. With each day that the debt is left outstanding, the higher the finance charges will be.

In general, the average daily balance method used by the bank card companies is about 16 percent more costly than the closing balance method used by many other creditors. Unfortunately, the companies using this second method usually charge a higher rate of interest. Each consumer has to examine his or her own particular case to find out which costs less.

Freeloaders on the Credit Card System

Advertising for credit cards stresses their convenience. Buy what you want, when you want it; get cash if you need it. No need for a loan application. Pay off your bill each month if you wish.

Advertising for credit cards does not tell you what the bankers really have in mind. They want you to borrow money and they do not want to have to process a loan application each time you buy something on credit, because that costs them $50. The reason is quite simple. Credit card systems can be very profitable for the banks, provided most people do not pay off their bills immediately. Unfortunately for the banks, over a third of the people using the cards are convenience users. That means they pay off their balances during the grace period and—to make matters worse—these ungrateful card users economize by delaying payments as long as possible. The banks claim that they cannot be profitable under these circumstances.

Payment Services, a textbook of the Bank Administration Institute in the United States claimed, "There is a growing feeling among banks that their credit card customers are using their cards strictly as convenience instruments rather than interest-bearing credit instruments. Customers are mainly deferring payments at the bank's expense, and the bank is confronted with a situation of high outstandings in receivables for which no income is being generated. A partial solution to this problem has been offered by a St. Louis banker. An annual fee may be necessary because the public is using charge cards more for convenience than for the deferred payment feature which results in the payment of interest to the card-issuing bank."[6]

One of the first banks to put this idea into effect was Citibank of New York. In the spring of 1976, it instituted a $.50 monthly charge on holders of its Master Charge card who did not borrow. "So why is big, smart Citibank charging a fee?" asked *Forbes,* a business publication.

> Explains a top executive: "We want to make the freeloaders pay." (In the curious language of our credit economy, a "freeloader" is someone who pays promptly, thus depriving the bank of interest.)[7]

Curious is right. Naturally the banks want you to borrow at 21 percent. Avoid it whenever you can.

When a Consumer Should Not Have a Credit Card

Having a credit card can affect consumers emotionally or lead them to spend without really considering the consequences. Ask people why they use credit cards and in too many instances they will give the worst of all possible reasons. A hockey player says he likes his credit card because he "can walk into the most expensive restaurant and order anything in the place." A young teacher says, "I can travel all over the world on my holidays for nothing."

Some people get a charge out of just having a credit card. It makes them feel important or special. It makes them forget the day of reckoning—the day when they slump in to face the facts of life with their bank manager.

> Mrs. O'Reilly is the manager of a bank in a well-to-do suburb of a big city. She has some horrifying stories to tell about the misuse of credit cards and these experiences have led her to question seriously their widespread use. "You wouldn't believe the number of people I see that use credit cards like they were a bottomless pit of money. Then one day they find that they have used up all their credit and they come to me to combine all their debt into one big loan.
>
> "I used to work out an arrangement for them to do this and I hoped that they had learned something from the experience.

Then I found out what most of them did. As soon as their debt
to the credit card company was paid off with the bank loan,
they went right out and started charging more things on their
credit cards. I have seen this happen so often that I won't loan
money anymore if it is just being used to refinance credit card
bills."

Any consumer who thinks that this example of irresponsible money management fits him should get out all his
credit cards and a pair of scissors, cut them through the
card number and into four pieces and put them into the
garbage. He won't regret it. As the Consumers' Association
of Canada said, "Credit can be a loyal servant if used
wisely; it becomes a destructive force to those who are
beguiled by its ready accessibility."[8]

Consumer Difficulties with Credit Cards

Bank credit cards can create problems for people who
do not use them as they should be used. They also can
create problems in many other ways because of our inade-
quate laws, the power of the banks, and errors in the system.

Difficulties in Obtaining a Credit Card

People can get a bank credit card easily if they are male,
have a steady job, earn over $200 a week, own a home and
a car, and already have a credit card. They may be refused
one if they are underage, retired, a housewife, recently
divorced, separated, or widowed, or earn a minimal income, although they may have assets and a responsible
financial history.

Mrs. Fairley was going on a holiday to the West Indies and thought it would be handy to have a MasterCard card. Then she would not have to tie up so much money in travellers cheques or worry about running out of money.

MasterCard did not think it was such a good idea. They turned her down because they said she did not have enough income. This was a poor reason on two grounds. Visa gave her a card without question, so her rating was satisfactory to them. She also had far more credit points than required by her bank for a good rating. She was a widow, owned a house, a cottage, and a car, lived adequately and responsibly on $600 a month, and had four department store credit cards, two oil company cards, and both a chequing and a savings account. All these items would produce a rating that was well above the minimum.

Mrs. Fairley was not the first and she will not be the last person to be turned down for a credit card because she did not fit the mould for the stereotype of the most desirable cardholder—the big spender. For her, there was a relatively easy solution. She could have spoken to her bank manager and it would have been arranged quickly. But, as she said, "I don't like to have to make waves so I didn't do anything about it."

The fact is that the credit card company should have made a better investigation of her credit worthiness. If credit cards are going to become essential equipment in the economic world of tomorrow, the card companies are going to have to deal more equitably with responsible people at all income levels.

Finally, a word of warning here to women who have never had a credit card with their own number. If you presently have a joint account with your husband and your credit cards both have the same number, you could be in serious trouble if you become widowed, separated, or divorced. You will find that your card is no longer valid and, what's more, you may have difficulty getting a new one because you have no credit rating of your own. The solution of course is to have your own card with its own number and to establish your own credit rating now before you need it.

Monthly Statements—Errors, Omissions, and Delayed Delivery

Your cardholder agreement holds you responsible for all authorized use of your card and this may include anything in the bank's records, right or wrong. The Instabank MasterCard Agreement states, "Bank records shall be conclusive and binding on all parties." In other words, the banks can do no wrong. But this is not always the case. Some mistakes are almost inevitable in a huge computer system and there may even be more than there should be in the credit card system.

"Billing errors," according to the Consumers' Association of Canada in their submission to the Standing Committee on Health, Welfare and Social Affairs,

> . . . have been a widespread source of complaint, though it must be added that some card issuers and grantors of variable credit have a much better record than others. A survey conducted in Toronto in 1975 on behalf of the Toronto branch of CAC and co-sponsored by the Consumer Research Council revealed that 48.2% of the respondents recalled having found a billing error and that only in 61.4% of the cases was the error corrected within a month to the consumer's satisfaction. 29.6% of the respondents indicated (contrary to the credit grantors' claim) that interest was being charged pending investigation of the consumer's complaint. Only a small percentage of the consumers interviewed reported having received any let-

ter or other form of explanation arising out of their complaint.[9]

Companies that issue credit cards can get away with this behaviour because a cardholder who finds an error in his statement is in a very weak legal position. Short of taking legal action, there is often nothing he can do about it.

The manager of a bank discovered a $20 error in his account with a credit card company. He notified the company but nothing was done about it. The next month, interest was charged on the $20. The card issuer could still not produce any evidence that the $20 was owed to them but they continued to ignore the complaint. This put the bank manager in a difficult position. In his job, he must have a clear credit record. That meant that his only alternatives were to sue the card issuer or pay the $20 plus interest charges. He paid.

Another serious and growing problem involves merchants failing to report promptly on returned goods, the cancellation or reduction of a debt, or other credit adjustments.

On March 2, 1978, a Master Charge account holder bought a railway ticket on the Canadian National Railways and charged $101.50 on her account. Three days later, she had to cancel the train reservation. The cancellation was not put through the account by the time it had to be paid. Consequently, the account holder had to pay that amount and did so on May 15, 1978. The account was finally credited with $101.50 on August 4, 1978, almost five months after the ticket was cancelled.

Situations like this mean that the cardholder must pay for the returned goods until the merchant's voucher is received by the card company. The cardholder should have the right to credit the merchant's adjustments to correct this problem, but at present only the merchant can do this.

In practice, cardholders have found that if they deduct their credits when making their payments, they will not be charged interest.

Cardholders may also be penalized unfairly because the statement does not arrive in the mail within a reasonable time. The cardholder may be charged interest on an account even though the account never arrived by the due date. In the United States, the Fair Credit Billing Act requires statements to be mailed fourteen days in advance of the due date.

People who live far away from the central computer of their charge card company can anticipate having mail problems in Canada. But this does not explain why payments made in a bank that is advertised as being connected by computer to its head office should take up to two weeks to spin along the computer network. One payment made in a Vancouver branch of the Bank of Montreal apparently went by mail, instead of computer, to central Canada. In this instance the cardholder in Vancouver had to pay up at least a week before a cardholder in Toronto in order to end interest charges on an "overdue" account.

Nels Jensen, a lawyer in Nelson, B.C., became incensed over this kind of situation and sued the Toronto-Dominion Bank over an $88.61 interest overcharge. He paid his Visa bill promptly each month but the bank did not credit his account until up to two weeks after each payment. In handing down his decision, Judge L. J. Keller found the bank guilty of misinterpreting its own credit card contract by repeatedly overcharging interest on bill payments. Jensen got $88.61 plus 1 percent interest. Coincidentally, the B.C. government ordered all banks to credit payments for charge card customers on the day that they are made at the bank. This has resulted in the banks noti-

fying their customers that payments will be credited immediately.

Liability for Unauthorized Use

Credit cards are frequently lost or stolen. This can happen through no fault of the cardholder, but all too often it
happens through carelessness. Cardholders should be particularly careful when they are travelling or if they have to
let the card out of their sight.

A favourite trick of waiters in some restaurants is to take
away your card to prepare the bill, then substitute some
other card for yours. Who ever checks to see if the right
card is returned? Most people just put it away until they
want to use it again. That may be days later while the thief
has had a whale of a time using your card.

Another restaurant trick is to fudge on the amount of the
tip. Chuck Davis, a columnist in the Vancouver *Province*,
said that

> A colleague responds to an item here which told of a woman
> who discovered that a Richmond restaurant had added a tip to
> her Chargex slip after she had signed it (she'd left a cash tip).
> His experience was even sleazier. He wrote in a $5 tip and
> someone changed it to $8. He took the matter to the Van-
> couver police fraud squad, who reported back that the "offend-
> ing party" had been "reprimanded." He started looking closer
> at his Master Charge receipts. The same thing happened at an-
> other restaurant. In both cases, he got refunds. Now he always
> checks. His note prompts me to change my habits. If I leave a
> written tip, it'll be like this: $3 (THREE). If I leave a cash
> tip, I'll write GIVEN in the tip line . . . Good advice.[10]

There is no law limiting your liability on a card in Canada but there should be. Both Visa and MasterCard

do state in their cardholder agreements that your liability for unauthorized use is limited to $50 if you notify them promptly that the card has been lost or stolen. Notification must be by phone or cable immediately followed up in writing. The Bank of Montreal protects the cardholder even more by stating that they will not penalize any Master-Card holder for any loss if they are notified quickly.

These are reasonable provisions which appear to work satisfactorily, but all credit card companies should be required to follow a similar policy. Legal limitations have been imposed in the United States to standardize and clarify the obligations of both cardholders and creditors.

Problems with Defective Merchandise

Your cardholder agreement says that the bank is not responsible for any disputes between a cardholder and a merchant and that these disputes can have no effect on the money you owe the bank. If you buy something that is defective, you must still pay the bank in full until the merchant turns in a credit slip.

Jenny Lee bought a pair of Austrian hiking boots from a sports store for $95 and paid for them with her credit card. The sales clerk assured her that the boots were a correct fit. Jenny climbed the Lions that weekend and collected two huge blisters. She took the boots back to the store and the clerk tried stretching them. The next weekend, Jenny lost four toenails coming down from the Black Tusk meadows. She took them back to the store again but the clerk refused to do anything this time. The manager backed him up and refused to take the boots back on the ground that they had been worn. When her credit card statement showed the charge next month, she had no alternative. She had to pay even though it was quite apparent that the boots had been fitted poorly and were of no use to her.

The problem here is that the bank is a third party to the sale and claims it has no responsibility for items bought with a credit card if they later turn out to be defective or are otherwise unsatisfactory. Both MasterCard and Visa state this very clearly in their cardholder agreements.

This puts the consumer in the same weak position as a cash customer. You cannot withhold payment or stop a cheque as you might do if you were dealing directly with a merchant. You must pay up and then you can go to court with the hope of getting your money plus interest. Sensing the unfairness of this situation, the Fair Credit Billing Act in the United States gave cardholders the right to withhold payments without being liable for the entire amount owing, but it applies only to purchases of more than $50 made in the buyer's state or within a hundred miles of the buyer's home. Canadian customers also need at least that amount of legal protection.

Misleading Advertising

The promotional literature put out by the bank charge card companies and their participating banks is often misleading or at least guilty of leaving out some significant facts. For this reason, it should be examined in the light of recent changes in the Federal Combines Investigation Act. Misleading advertising covered by the act now includes the general presentation of advertising as well as specific details relating to it. There is also a technical amendment to the effect that the "general impression test" can be used in court to assess whether or not the whole representation is misleading.

The package accounts like the Commerce Key Account offer a wide range of services for a monthly fee but in the advertising, the banks do not say that you have to fill out an application for a bank credit card when you apply for the package account—even though you do not want one. I told an employee at the Royal Bank that I did not want a credit card but she insisted that I apply for one, then I could cut it up if I did not want it. The banks' excuse for requiring a credit card is that customers authorize a credit check on themselves when applying for a credit card, and this makes it easier for everybody if customers apply for a loan on any preferred terms allowed to package holders.

Most applications for a credit card include a cardholder agreement setting out the terms on which the credit card is issued. The Commerce, however, provides a Visa application without the cardholder agreement—the fine detail where the bank has the hammerlock—but setting out very well the advantages to a cardholder. Furthermore, the applicant agrees to abide by the terms of the cardholder agreement without ever seeing one. An application form signed without the bank first providing the cardholder agreement should be legally invalid.

Many consumers would benefit from a clearer explanation of the manner in which credit charges are calculated, and from a statement stating how long it will take to pay off their loan at the minimum monthly payment.

In this area as in many others, the banks are under no real pressure to change their ways. Advertising comes under the purview of the Department of Consumer and Corporate Affairs, a weak department, while banking is regulated by Finance, a strong arm of government with no interest in consumer matters.

The Real Costs of Credit Cards to the Economy

Ralph Nader told the National Commission on Consumer Finance in the United States, "Anyone engaged in consumer (price) protection is a hypocrite if he has a credit card. I won't have a credit card because it increases the cost of things to everyone."[11] Many people agree with Nader that there is such a thing as credit card inflation and they point to ways in which they believe prices are raised to cover the added costs of credit cards.

Under the present system, credit cards are free to the cardholder. Therefore, someone else must pay for the transaction costs of goods and services bought with a credit card. This is generally the merchant who accepts the credit. A store must rent an imprinter at $12 a year (although the same one can be used for both bank cards). MasterCard requires the merchant to also pay a percentage of the sale which varies between 5½ and 2 percent, depending on the monthly volume of the store and the amount of the individual sale. The Visa maximum is 5¾ percent.

As an offset to these costs, the merchant does not have to pay the expenses of running his own credit operation, although in most cases this is not likely to be a big cost factor. The merchant may also gain added business by making credit card sales and so lower his unit costs. There are no well-documented studies to prove the case either way.

If prices are raised to cover the added costs, prices will be raised for all consumers regardless of whether they pay by cash, cheque, or credit card. The very occasional merchant will give the cash customer a discount from the regular price but the practice is not encouraged by charge card companies, as this extract from *Chargex Bulletin* shows.

A statement about cash discounts

You're probably aware of the quiet controversy surrounding cash discounts. There have been some suggestions that merchants should pass on the equivalent of the merchant discount for charge or credit cards to customers who choose to pay cash. Clause number two in the Chargex Merchant's Member Agreement now reads: "Upon presentation of a Chargex Card by a Cardholder or an Authorized User, the Merchant agrees to sell merchandise to or perform services for the account of Cardholder at the same prices and upon the same conditions as those applicable to cash transactions."

The clause is not intended or interpreted by the Chargex banks to mean that merchants are prohibited from granting discounts to customers electing to pay cash. The purpose of this clause is to ensure that users of the Chargex card are required to pay no more than the listed price for goods and services which they buy. To ensure against misinterpretation of the position of the Chargex Plan on this subject, the wording of the clause will be clarified for future issues of the Merchant's Member Agreement.[12]

The large majority of merchants who charge identical prices are, no matter what the method of payment, passing the transaction costs of the credit card sales on to the cash user. Therefore the pricing system is not acting efficiently because the cardholder is not paying directly for the convenience of using the credit card.

A second economic issue in the credit card debate involves the free credit given to the cardholders from the date of a purchase to the date of a payment. One study by the Economic Council of Canada estimates that the implicit interest paid on Chargex and Master Charge varies from 2 to 3 percent.[13]

If costs such as implicit interest and some of the merchant's discount were paid directly by the cardholder, it would force consumers to recognize the issues involved. As the study mentioned previously points out, "This division of charges should eliminate any illusions on the part of the cardholders that the use of the card or the credit provided prior to payment are 'free.' They would then be confronted with the costs of alternative methods of payment and their choice would more nearly reflect the economic costs involved."[14]

Another important issue for the economy is the whole question of control and access given to the bank credit card system. The chartered banks control the bank card system which gives them an enormous competitive advantage over other deposit-taking institutions. Credit cards have proved to be both an important profit centre through the revenues earned on the unpaid balances and a way to extend banking services into new areas. Other financial institutions are denied access to the existing system unless they pay an entrance fee, and at the same time they are deterred from initiating another system by the huge costs of entering the business.

The Economic Council of Canada is strongly opposed to this monopoly position and recommended in 1976 that "all deposit institutions be assured access to existing bank card systems through compulsory licensing on terms that are non-discriminatory to both existing card issuers and to the entering institutions."[15]

A fourth question involves the impact of credit cards on the amount and the rate of consumer spending. One study indicates that consumers buy 13 percent more on the average than they would if they did not have credit cards.[16] By making it easier to buy and to secure credit, cards encourage consumers to spend more freely, and so money passes around the economic system at a faster rate. This increased velocity of money can be inflationary.

Recent information from the United States also points out the dangerous potential of this increased spending when it leads to an overload of consumer debt. Delinquencies and loan losses on credit cards are soaring in the States. The *Wall Street Journal* estimated in 1979 that more than $810 million of Visa and Master Charge loans were behind in their payments by thirty days or more. This was a 75 percent increase over arrears of $460 million in 1978. In addition, the banks wrote off over $2.00 of every $100 owed them on Master Charge accounts, while Visa wrote off $1.80 on every $100.

The *Wall Street Journal* attributed much of this debt problem to the banks for their mass marketing of credit cards and their lowering of credit standards. But part of the blame must go to consumers for their addiction to credit cards and borrowing as a way of life. The *Journal* gave this story as an example:

> With a combined income of $18,000 and a spotless credit history, Mr. and Mrs. John D. were valued customers of the Midwestern bank. So when the couple used up their credit line on their Visa card, the bank was more than willing to raise their borrowing limit.
>
> But after running up a $2,000 bill on the card earlier this year, the couple shocked the bank by filing for personal bankruptcy. Even more of a surprise were the disclosures on the bankruptcy petition. The couple had been using 17 other cards from banks, oil companies and department stores. The total tab: $32,000.
>
> "It was a classic case of trying to borrow their way out of financial problems," says an official of the bank. "They built a house of plastic cards and it all came tumbling down."[17]

Credit cards can also lead to serious problems for governments and central banks in their attempts to manipulate the economy through their control of bank liabilities. Because holders of credit cards use cash less frequently and maintain smaller chequing accounts, there is less demand for money but an increase in its velocity. As one commentator expressed it, "The problem with monetary policy in a credit card world is that this linchpin of monetary policy, the reserve ratio, has been knocked away."[18]

Credit cards, in the view of bankers, are an interim and useful phase in the evolution of the chequeless society. That is the essential reason why the banks have been pushing the use of credit cards in recent years. Happily for the banks, credit cards have also proved to be very profitable. It is less clear how the consumer benefits or how government will protect them.

The Honourable André Ouellet, Minister of Consumer and Corporate Affairs, said in a speech to the Consumer Law Protection Conference, on September 26, 1975, that "a revolution is underway in Canada which will transform this country from a paper-based system of currency and cheques . . . to a society with no cash at all." At the same time he called on all parts of society to participate in planning for such a system. Unfortunately, the debate, which has been carried on largely among the government, the banks, and the computer industry, has concerned itself mainly with the technology and economic efficiency of the electronic funds transfer system. There has been very little discussion of the wants and needs of the consumer.

First of all, credit cards need to be recognized legally; there is no general legislation at this time on the subject of credit cards. The closest any government has come to this subject is to pass laws in most of the provinces which make the card issuer, not the cardholder, responsible for unsolicited cards (cards sent to a consumer who has not applied for them). Apart from that, the credit card is not recognized by the law specifically, a situation that can only play into the hands of the banks and leave the consumer unprotected from error, fraud, or misrepresentation.

13

How Safe Is a Safety Deposit Box
or Securities in Safekeeping?

In July of 1976, one of the most spectacular robberies in French history took place in the heart of the French Riviera. A branch of the Société Générale bank in Nice was robbed of more than $10 million by a six-member gang who tunnelled into the vault, rifled the deposit boxes, and escaped through sewers in a rubber dinghy. This was the biggest vault robbery since the record-breaking $14 million taken from a German bank in 1945.

Vancouver had its own wild vault robbery when $2.5 million was stolen from the Vancouver Safety Deposit Vault Company in January 1977. This was not the first robbery from this vault. A Delta, B.C., couple charged that two bags of silver coins worth $5,000 had been placed in a locked metal box and stored in the strong-room of this company in 1975. One year later, when they returned to the vault to examine their valuables, they discovered that their inflationary hedge had been transformed into two clay bricks wrapped in plastic bags.

In the big theft, thieves drilled through a cement wall to gain entrance to the vault, then broke open about 1,200 safety deposit boxes. They lugged away $280,000 in cash, $300,000 worth of gold, and $1 to $1.5 million in coins and jewellery, but they only got as far as Vancouver airport. An alert baggage handler wondered why the bags were so heavy and called the police, who arrested two men. Three others charged with the robbery were later picked up in Winnipeg.

This episode was a great revelation to all the people who not only thought that safety deposit boxes were safe, but also that the company or financial institution that was renting them had some legal obligations in case of theft. The facts are quite different. Safety deposit boxes are protected from theft in varying degrees that depend on how well the vault is constructed and how well it is guarded when it is open.

Like nearly every other situation in life, it is probably correct to say that no safety deposit box is 100 percent secure from theft. Ingenious bank robbers have frequently proven that. Given that fact, it is important to look at the fine print in the safety deposit box rental agreement which most people sign when they rent a box. It will usually say something to this effect.

> *Loss or Damage:* The customer agrees that both after as well as before the expiration or termination of this Agreement until the Customer has surrendered the Box the liability of the Bank shall be limited to the exercise of ordinary diligence to prevent the opening of the Box by any person other than the Customer or the duly authorized representative of the Customer. Such opening shall not be presumed from proof of partial or total loss of the contents. Without limiting the generality of the

foregoing, the Customer agrees that the Bank shall not be liable for loss or damage occasioned by fire, theft or any other causes.

Cleared of the legalese, this means that you have no legal protection for anything placed in this safety deposit box unless you can prove conclusively that the bank allowed someone access to your box and that that person was proved to have removed something valuable from it. Just finding that it has been cleaned out will not help you and it could be very difficult—and expensive—to prove that the bank was negligent.

The only real protection you can have in this case is insurance. You should insure the contents of your box if it holds anything that is very valuable and can be sold easily, like uncut diamonds, gold coins, or bearer bonds.

How Not to Use Safety Deposit Boxes

Someone did not like the Bank of Montreal very much. He rented a safety deposit box, locked a package in it, and went for a long holiday in Europe. After a few days, the box began to smell. After a few weeks, the whole vault reeked. The bank employees could not find the person who rented the box. Finally they drilled out the lock and removed the stinking package containing, of all things, a very dead fish.

Trust officers collect stories of things they have found in safety deposit boxes after people have died. Pornography or incriminating photographs are a favourite. The bereaved widow attends the opening of her deceased husband's box expecting to find bond certificates and a copy of his will. Instead, she finds several pictures of her husband disporting himself with frisky ladies.

A more common situation is the one where the only copy of the will and the burial instructions are in a safety deposit box. It cannot be opened over a long weekend or until some legal formalities are completed. In the meantime, somebody must dispose of the body.

If you are sharing a box with someone and he or she dies, the box is locked up until the proper leases are signed. The moral—own your own. DO not share one just to save $9.50 a year.

The Convenience of Safekeeping

If you want more security and convenience—at a price —you might consider leaving your stocks and bonds in the care of a banking institution.

These safekeeping or custody arrangements are a great convenience and a better choice than a safety deposit box for many people. There is no problem making payment or delivery if you are out of town; you do not have to go to your safety deposit box every time you buy or sell a security. Investors with large portfolios, estate executors, guardians, and trustees can be relieved of a lot of paperwork.

The procedure is simple. The bank or trust company holds the bonds, stocks, or mortgages in its own vault and will clip coupons or receive interest and dividend cheques if you wish. When securities are sold, the bank will release them on your instructions at either settlement date or the payment date. Conversely, the bank will make payments for purchases of securities on either the settlement date or the delivery date.

All banks and trust companies dealing with the general public provide these services, and there seem to be only minor differences in the quality of the services provided. It is a generally satisfactory method, though it is advisable to check on the bank regularly since errors come up in every account from time to time.

The charges for these services at trust companies appear to be fairly uniform. Usually the charge is based on a percentage of the market value of the portfolio. The percentage decreases at intervals as the portfolio increases. There is a minimum charge (which banks don't have) that makes a custody arrangement with a trust company uneconomic for portfolios with a market value of much less than $200,000.

Canada Permanent, for instance, advertises this fee schedule for safekeeping and collection of income:

⅜ of 1 percent on the first $250,000 (minimum fee $375);
¼ of 1 percent on the next $500,000; and
⅛ of 1 percent over $750,000.

These rates work out to charges of $375 for a $100,000 portfolio and $2,500 for a $1 million portfolio.

The banks have a different system, and it varies between banks, but the most common method is to assess bonds at a certain percentage of their par value. Stock, and sometimes bonds, are assessed at a certain percentage of their income if the bank collects the income, or at a fixed fee per certificate if it does not collect the income. There is also a charge in most banks for the delivery of certificates.

These are the rates quoted to knowledgeable investors. Other investors pay a lot more because a bank can charge any rate the traffic will bear. You cannot count on the bank to quote the best rate that you can get.

An investor with a portfolio worth about $12 million had a safekeeping arrangement with a bank which was cov-

When the banks handle the income they charge these fees:

	Bank of Montreal	Toronto-Dominion Bank	Bank of British Columbia
BONDS	---------- % ----------------		
Up to $100,000 par value	0.30	0.30	0.25
$100,000 to $1 million	0.15	0.15	0.125
$1 million to $6 million	0.08	0.08	0.0625
Over $6 million	0.06	0.06	0.05
STOCKS	---------- % ----------------		
Up to $5,000 income	6	6	5
$5,000 to $50,000	3	3	2.5
$50,000 to $300,000	1.5	1.5	1.25
Over $300,000	1.25	1.25	1

When the banks do not handle the income, or there is no income, they charge these fees:

	Bank of Montreal	Toronto-Dominion Bank	Bank of British Columbia
BONDS	---------- % ----------------		
Up to $100,000 par value	0.15	0.15	0.125
$100,000 to $1 million	0.08	0.075	0.0625
$1 million to $6 million	0.04	0.04	0.03125
Over $6 million	0.03	0.03	0.025
		($2.50 certificate if fully registered)	
	$1 per certificate per year	$1 per certificate per year	75¢ per certificate per year

Delivery charges at banks are:

Bank of Montreal	Toronto-Dominion Bank	Bank of British Columbia
0.001% of market value	$7.50 an entry	over 1 entry per year—$2.00 per certificate

ered by the typical safekeeping agreement stating that the charges will be the normal, reasonable rates for that type of account. The investor was charged 2 percent of his income, which was over $300,000. Foolishly, no check was made on these charges and it was paid for several years.

A new investment advisor was horrified to see this rate because it was double the rate the investor should have been charged. The regular rate charged by that bank for that type of service was 1 percent. The investment advisor pointed this out to the bank and it agreed to negotiate a settlement of the overcharges for the previous year. "But," said the manager, "you have to realize that any settlement will mostly come out of the pay of a bank employee." The investment advisor did not go for that kind of blackmail because it certainly was not true and the full amount was awarded to the investor. In addition, a new safekeeping agreement was signed with specific rates which were the same as the bank quoted publicly.

In another instance, a retired couple asked an investment counsellor to handle their portfolio and use the safekeeping facilities of the bank which they had dealt with for over thirty years. The bank insisted over and over again that the regular rate for this type of service was 3 percent of the income, regardless of whether it came from bonds or stocks. The investment counsellor questioned this rate several times because the other banks charged one type of rate on bonds and one type on stocks. Next the counsellor found out that this bank in fact did have a schedule of rates identical to the schedule quoted by the Bank of Montreal and the Toronto-Dominion. The bank was overcharging by 60 percent.

From these two examples, you can see that every investor with a safekeeping account should check out the rates very carefully to be sure they are reasonable and fair. The bank may not tell you if you don't ask.

What Is the Bank's Liability on Safekeeping?

The bank's liability for anything held in safekeeping is quite different from their liability towards renters of safety deposit boxes. In legal parlance, the relationship between a bank and their customer resulting from the deposit of securities with it for safekeeping is considered that of bailor and bailee. This means that the very thing deposited must be returned to the depositor and, in order to carry out this obligation, the bank must use ordinary care and diligence in holding securities for safekeeping. However, there is no liability as an insurer, as there is none with safety deposit boxes. Therefore the bank is only liable for loss resulting from its failure to exercise care required by law. Should the bank fail to provide modern vaults, adequate police protection, and the use of protective devices, then it may be liable. The other types of risk are insured by the bank under its bankers' blanket bond to cover employee theft, fraud, damage, or burglary.

In essence, the legal position of an investor placing securities in safekeeping is quite strong. The bank will provide a record of all stocks and bonds left with them or released by them. In the event that the bank loses any, it will cover any loss as a public relations measure. The only disadvantages are the errors in accounts, the cost, and the fact that safekeeping is designed only for holding investment securities like bonds or shares. Your other precious possessions like gold, silver, jewellery, and legal documents must be held in your safety deposit box.

14

Banks, Trust Companies, and Credit Unions as Financial Advisors

Nearly everybody in Canada needs financial advice. What to do with your savings? How do you keep down your taxes? How do you plan for your retirement or the inevitable rainy day? What do you do with your winnings if you hit the jackpot? Where do you go for reliable, competent, and impartial financial advice for problems like this?

The answer to the financial advisor conundrum, for most Canadians, is to go to their bank, trust company, or credit union. A survey prepared in 1979 for the British Columbia Resources Investment Corporation indicated that people do this by an overwhelming margin. This corporation was preparing to sell the largest stock issue ever proposed in British Columbia and it wanted to get the widest and most successful distribution.

Generally, shares of new issues like this are sold through

investment dealers, but BCRIC wanted to reach people who never think of buying shares or going to an investment dealer or stockbroker. It wanted to find out where these people went for investment advice and it found out that they had an overwhelming preference. The survey reported that more than half the people questioned would go to a bank, a trust company, or a credit union for financial advice. About 20 percent would go to friends and a meagre 19 percent would ask an investment dealer or stockbroker. That certainly says very little for the professional purveyors of investment advice but it is easy to understand.

Customers are used to visiting their bank, seeing bank employees handle money, and reading about the different kinds of savings accounts and investments that banks offer. They may even have talked to the manager when they wanted a loan. From this accumulated experience, a lot of people come away with the idea that they can get reliable, impartial financial advice at their bank.

What most people do not know or seem to understand is that all too often they get incompetent and extremely partial financial advice. Employees of banks, trust companies, and credit unions are rarely trained adequately to provide good advice. They are there to sell the products of that particular financial institution and not to provide comparisons with other institutions or other types of investments which may be unfavourable to that bank. It all boils down to the fact that, in most cases, financial advice is not and should not be their business. This fact is quite apparent at every level of the organization.

To give an example of what happens at the lowest level, the investment manager of a trust company was concerned with the manner in which his staff at branch offices handled the latest Canada Savings Bond issue, so he decided to go around to several of the offices to check. The people in each branch who were selling the bonds to the customers had been sent information about the new issue and had also been sent information about previous issues to help them advise people on the suitability of turning in their old bonds on the new issue. An adequate time after the staff had received this material, the manager checked to see how they were using it.

At branch after branch, he heard the same thing, "I asked them if they had read the material and if they had understood it," he said, "and I was appalled to find out that they had just stuck it under the counter to read later. Quite a few could not even find where they had put it."

This attitude to providing good financial advice is not confined to the lowest levels in a bank either—as many people have found out to their considerable regret. Very few managers are equipped to provide good investment advice.

Hilary Cornish inherited $20,000 in Canada Savings Bonds from her father. They had been bought over a period of six years so each one was slightly different. The interest rates were not the same, some had bonus payments for compound interest, and the maturities varied. She did not know whether she should hold on to them, turn them into the new issue, or buy a different type of security, and she had no experience in making investment decisions. It seemed only natural to her to ask her bank manager what she should do with these bonds.

That should have been an easy task for anyone qualified to give investment advice to the public. CSBs are sold in multiples of $100 at a fixed price of $100 and will be bought back by the government at that same price plus interest whenever a holder of the bonds takes them to a bank, trust company, credit union, or investment dealer. The interest rate is fixed when the bonds are sold but the rate usually changes each year. When the level of interest rates in Canada was low in 1966 the rate was set at 5 to 6 percent. When rates were high in 1974, the interest rate was increased to 9.75 percent. When this happens, holders of low-yielding bonds are advised to sell their bonds and buy the higher yielding bonds to improve their income.

That is exactly the advice that Hilary received from the bank manager in November 1978. The government was selling CSBs paying interest at 9.5 percent and Hilary was told to sell her bonds paying 6 percent and buy the new bonds. A good deal for Hilary—her income would increase. And a good deal for the bank manager—he would earn a commission on the sale.

Sounds like a good idea for everybody. But Hilary should have looked a little closer. If she had, she would have found out that her bonds were maturing in one year, in November 1979. At that time she would get back the full face value of the bonds. She understood that but what she, and apparently her bank manager, didn't know was that she would also get a cash bonus of $30.35 for every $100 bond. This bonus raised the interest rate on her bonds to 36.75 percent, and she lost it all when she sold them on her bank manager's advice.

This is not an isolated or rare example of the kind of advice that people receive from banks, trust companies, or credit unions. It is a common occurrence. It is also a predictable occurrence because people giving out advice over the counter are, with rare exceptions, not qualified to advise people about their personal finances. They have little or no training and often make no effort to acquire the knowledge to provide the advice competently.

Investment Advice

Advising on CSBs is relatively simple. What happens to people who want advice on other bonds, stocks, or term deposits? These securities have to be integrated into the whole financial picture for each individual and they should only be sold by people who are trained and experienced in advising the public on investments. The average employee of a bank, trust company, or credit union has only the most minimal knowledge in this field. At higher levels, employees do receive some training in the management of investments. Bank employees can take courses through the educational arm of the Canadian Bankers' Association, and trust company employees can do the same through the Canadian Institute of Trust Companies.

But a semester course in investments only opens the door; it doesn't provide any real understanding of the investment process. To begin with, the investment process has become incredibly complex in recent years. The range of choices has become enormous and even within limited categories it is quite large.

But choice is not the only complicating factor. Taxes have to be considered. Should the investor be deferring taxes on his income through an RHOSP or RRSP? Do some kinds of shares give a better income after taxes than a bond as a result of new tax legislation? Should the investor use cash to pay off the mortgage on his home and then borrow money for investing to take advantage of the tax deductibility of interest payments on money borrowed to earn income? Has the married investor looked at the advantages of income splitting?

All these factors have to be taken into consideration when you get financial advice, and there is no way that you will get good advice unless you get it from a financial counsellor with a great deal of knowledge and experience. The whole situation becomes almost ludicrous when you consider that a bank manager can advise anyone on investments without any training or licensing or regulations, but a sales representative of an investment dealer must pass examinations, receive a thorough checking by the RCMP and the Securities Commission, and complete the training program of his company before he can advise anyone on investments.

On the surface there would seem to be a simple answer to this problem. Pay to have money managed and you get good advice. Your money will then earn a reasonable amount and will be managed wisely to protect its value. Taxes will be kept to a minimum. Money won't be left idly sitting in chequing accounts. It will be invested competently in the best mix of securities in line with each person's need for income, security, liquidity, and capital gain. This is the ideal of sound financial management, but can most consumers attain it?

Individual financial management is expensive because it takes a great deal of time and it requires competent (and therefore well-paid) people to provide it. The wealthy person can get it from financial planners, some lawyers, investment counsellors, and trust companies. People with moderate income and assets cannot afford this service but they can turn to service provided by some credit unions or group meetings initiated by trust companies and credit unions. All investment dealers also provide a great deal of financial advice for no charge other than usual commissions on the sale or purchase of securities.

Money Managing by Trust Companies

Trust companies have the lion's share of the money managed by professionals for individual people. In 1980, they managed at least $64 billion in their trust accounts. Part of this money is held in trust accounts set up in people's wills or in trusts designed to protect large estates. Many people with more modest assets also left their estates in the hands of the trust company but this practice is dying out because trust companies do not want to handle accounts with a value of less than $100,000.

Another important part of this big pool of money is managed by trust companies under individual management contracts or agency agreements. These accounts must also be very large—in many cases at least $500,000.

The charges to manage these big investment portfolios depend basically on what type of account it is. A trust set up under a will, called a testamentary trust, is limited by law or regulation of the courts to around 5 percent of the capital of the account, 5 percent of the annual income and, in some provinces, to ¼ of 1 percent a year on the total value of the assets. Trust companies naturally prefer higher rates and try to convince the people involved with these trust accounts to agree to higher charges. The charge for a typical investment account is about ⅝ to ¾ of 1 percent a year on portfolios of $500,000 or less. This can add up to a lot of money year after year, but if the management is good it may be worth it; all too often it is not.

In November 1976, an heir to the Ritchie Estate charged that the Canada Trust mismanaged her grandfather's estate and brought on a loss of about $828,000 as a result of its administration. The trust company in turn asked for $292,000 as its costs for administering the estate. The total costs to the estate as a result of Canada Trust's management would then be $1,120,000 in lost capital.

Bad management of trust accounts is even more serious for smaller trusts. That does not mean just $25,000 accounts. It means any account worth less than $200,000. There are records of case after case of accounts of this size subjected to the most incredible abuses. The trustees act illegally and incompetently and charge punitive expenses against the trust. And there is little or no protection under our legal system against these abuses. The beneficiaries just have to accept whatever is done to them because they do not have the knowledge, the influence, and the money to fight the powerful trust companies.

A well-documented example of a small trust that was handled with incredible ineptitude is the I.F. Estate. A trust company managed it for four years after the settlor of the trust died. During that time, they made major investment decisions without consulting the cotrustee, lost a considerable amount of money for the beneficiaries by insisting on following incorrect legal advice, overcharged, made illiquid investments with no regard for imminent capital disposition, and lost stock certificates.

The beneficiaries took the trust company to the Surrogate Court of Ontario in an attempt to get some compensation for the financial losses they had suffered. The judge refused to give a decision in apparent violation of the Surrogate Court Act. The only options left for these beneficiaries were to move the case to the far more expensive Supreme Court or to try to settle out of court. In desperation they settled for a puny amount that in no way compensated them for their financial losses. They did succeed in getting the trust to pass the remnants of the trust assets to a competent trustee.

A common problem that beneficiaries of trusts mention is that their financial statements are prepared in a way that these people cannot understand and then they are pressured into signing a release that prevents a beneficiary from ever challenging the statements unless there is considerable error or fraud. The usual tactic is to tell the beneficiary that it will be very costly to do otherwise.

No trust account should ever be set up that gives a trust company effective control over the trust. Women should make sure that any trust that their husbands set up names them as coexecutrixes and cotrustees with the absolute power to change the trust company at any time if the arrangement is not satisfactory. Better still, they should learn enough about money management to be able to choose their own advisors.

The average person with a few thousand dollars in savings and some very basic budgeting, tax, or retirement problem is also at a loss for good financial advice. There are places where advice is given for free but in getting free advice, it is worthwhile to remember the old adage that advice is worth what you pay for it.

Vancouver City Savings Credit Union, as an example, lined up two retired chartered accountants to provide a free money advice service to its 100,000 members. Each counselling session lasts about three-quarters of an hour and covers a wide variety of topics. Taxes, RRSPs, Canada Savings Bonds, and term deposits are frequent subjects. This can be very helpful for some consumers but it has limitations. The credit union has a vested interest in selling these products and once again, the customers are often getting advice from people who are not trained or experienced in providing investment advice.

For average people who cannot afford expensive financial counselling, the question repeatedly comes back to the fact that they must do a lot of investigating themselves. They must comparison shop, and they must search out sources for relatively inexpensive investment advice. A good investment dealer is an obvious choice. Night-school courses can be very beneficial. Just don't rely completely on your friendly banker.

PART THREE

Banking in the Future

15

Electronic Funds
Transfer System

The Canadian banking system has changed more in the last ten years than in the previous fifty. The assets, power, and influence of the banking system have grown more rapidly; there are far more companies providing banking services; and behind all this lies the ubiquitous computer, which will change banking more in the next five years than it has changed in the last one hundred.

"Meanwhile back at the ranch," as they used to say on "Gunsmoke," are the consumers—usually ignored by the federal government whenever it comes to banking policy and usually unaware of new developments in banking which will have such a radical effect on them.

You can see how an electronic funds transfer system (EFTS) will affect you if you compare some simple financial transactions that you often make using the present system with how you will do it using an EFT system.

Start first with the procedure for withdrawing cash from

a bank. With the old system, you give a withdrawal slip to
the teller who either writes up the ledger card or manually
puts the information into a machine that prepares the
bank's ledgers. You may even have a friendly chat about
your account. At the end of the month you receive a statement reporting how much you have taken out of your account or put into it.

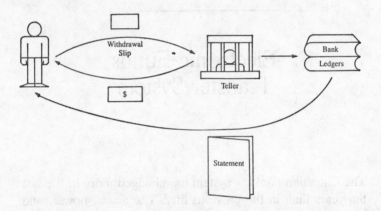

All this changes with EFTS. Now you have nobody to
talk to or ask questions, just a machine with slots and but-
tons. You push your plastic card into the machine, try to
find your personal identification number, which you have
hidden somewhere, push the button that tells the machine
to take out cash, punch the button that tells the machine
how much, take out your card, and collect your cash. While
all this is going on, the automatic teller is talking to a central computer about you. The computer knows that you are
No. 4444, that you have $60 in your chequing account,
and that you are taking out $25. It gives this information
to your branch bank and at the end of the month, you get a
statement telling you what you did. Very efficient (or so it

looks at first) and totally impersonal. Now you almost never have to go into a bank.

24-HOUR AUTOMATIC TELLER MACHINES

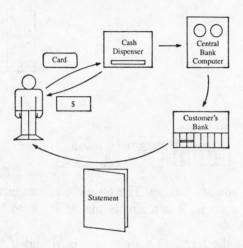

That is the simplest part of the electronic funds transfer system. It gets far more involved when extended to the checkout counter at your grocery or department store. The present system is based on you using cash, a cheque, or a credit card to pay for anything you buy. If you pay for your new winter coat with a cheque, the cycle will go like this. The cheque is deposited in the store's bank, sent to a clearing house to be sorted, sent to your bank for payment, and finally returned to you with your monthly statement.

What happens when a store joins the EFTS? Each checkout counter is equipped with a point-of-sale terminal. You fill up your basket with groceries and take them to the checkout. The automatic scanner reads all those strange lines on your cans and packages and tells the terminal ex-

PRESENT POINT-OF-SALE CHECK CYCLE

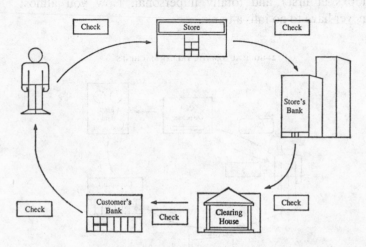

actly what you are buying. The terminal knows how much everything costs so it is a simple matter for it to burp up the total of $44.75.

You give the terminal your plastic card and it immediately talks to (or accesses, as the jargon goes) the computer at your bank. Being very suspicious, the computer asks who is handing in the card. You speak into a microphone which carries the sound to a machine that makes a voice print. The computer compares this new voice print with the voice print stored in your account, decides it is the same, and then checks your bank account to see if you really have $44.75. If you do, the computer takes the money out of your account and sends it to the bank where the store has its account. At the end of the month, your bank tells you that you are eating too many potato chips.

Sounds all very efficient. But what happens if you do not have enough money in your account or if you want to stop payment because the merchandise was defective? Tough luck.

EFT POINT-OF-SALE FUNDS TRANSFER SYSTEM USING A CENTRAL SWITCH

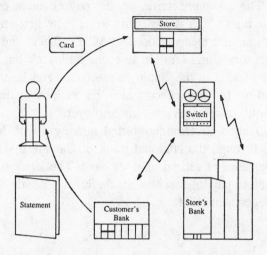

You will also meet EFTS when you get your pay cheque. Payrolls are a nuisance now because the employer has to make up a cheque with a statement of deductions for everybody, make sure everybody gets their cheques, and then reconcile the whole business when it lands back on his lap.

PRESENT PAYROLL CYCLE

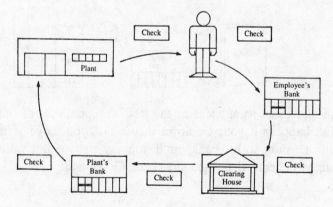

EFTS solves all these nagging problems—for the employer. The company writes up the payroll on a convenient little tape which is passed on to its bank first and then to an automatic clearing house (ACH). There the information is sorted and sent out to each employee's bank. The pay is deposited in the employee's account and he receives a statement to that effect which he verifies against the cheque stub he receives from his employer.

The Quebec government started making direct deposits like this through the National Bank of Canada in 1977 to cover pensions of retired civil servants. The Bank of Canada began to pay interest on Canada Savings Bonds through direct deposits in 1978.

DIRECT DEPOSIT

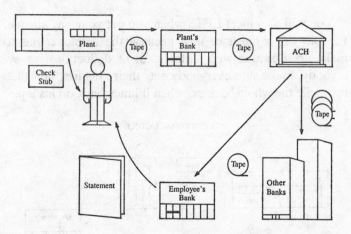

Sounds just as efficient as the new shopping system but what happens if your employer insists that you move your bank account to his bank, or if you say you do not want your pay cheque deposited anywhere. Good luck!

Pre-Authorized Payments

Some consumers use pre-authorized payments now to avoid the bother of writing the same cheque each month to make payments for insurance, mortgages, loans, or purchases of mutual funds. They can do this by issuing postdated cheques made payable to one organization in identical amounts but with a series of different payment dates. Or the consumer can sign a form authorizing the bank to collect money from the consumer's bank account in certain specific amounts on a regular basis to pay these bills.

In an electronic funds transfer system, this would be accomplished by the consumer authorizing the payment and the company which is owed the money preparing a tape. The computer would be told the names of everybody making payments, along with the amount each one owes, the date it is due, the numbers of the accounts from which it will be taken, and the names of banks holding the accounts.

Despite their growing use, pre-authorized debits are still looked at with suspicion or outright disfavour. A study by the Economic Council of Canada reported, "Most consumers feel that the benefits would be small, with the strongest advantage being the insurance such plans afford against forgetting to pay bills. The potential disadvantages are much more apparent to consumers. The major concern is that pre-authorized debit systems no longer allow them to control their finances with respect to the timing and amount of payment. Consumers also feel that merchants are more willing to make adjustments or to take back faulty or damaged merchandise when bills are unpaid. Some feel that the ability to delay payments temporarily can be a major benefit in making ends meet. Finally, they are afraid that both banks and merchants may make mistakes in the amounts charged and these are difficult if not impossible to rectify once they are locked into the system."[1]

This kind of payment is bound to increase despite objections by consumers because it is ideally suited to automation. An EFTS with its data banks, automatic clearing houses, and remote terminals lives by payment transactions like this. They will want all the business they can get so it is quite likely that some banking institutions will pressure unwilling individuals to pre-authorize their loan and mortgage payments as a condition for getting the loan.

The New Machines and What They Will Do for You

These different ways in which you will be involved in the EFTS mention new machines which you may not have seen or heard of before. They are all part of the huge computer network that will be required for the EFTS to link customers in stores, workers in factories, old-age pensioners, owners of businesses, and governments to the banking system. Through automatic teller machines (ATMs), point-of-sale terminals (POSs), automatic clearing houses (ACHs), personal identity verification (PIV), personal identification numbers (PINs), and plastic cards.

Automatic Teller Machines (ATMs)

ATMs are widely used in Great Britain, France, and Japan, and Canadian banks are increasing their use. We have Instabank at the Bank of Montreal, Instant Teller at the Commerce, and the Green Machine at the Toronto-Dominion. Their use here has been relatively slow to grow though because they are expensive to operate. Some American reports claim that it costs about $1.25 for every transaction using an ATM while it costs about $.35 for a transaction at the teller's wicket.

An ATM can provide many of the services of a bank teller. It can take in cash deposits, make cash withdrawals, transfer money between accounts, make cash advances against prearranged lines of credit, and pay bills from accounts. In addition, it can be located in airports, train stations, and other locations outside banks to give customers bank services outside normal bank hours. It accomplishes all this because it is connected to a central computer that immediately enters any transaction in a customer's account.

What can't an ATM do? It cannot cash a third-party cheque like a baby-bonus payment. It cannot update your passbook. It can't sell you travellers cheques or a money order.

The Credit/Payment Card

The plastic card is the entrée to the EFTS and it is a very different thing from the usual bank or department store credit card. With these familiar types of cards, a customer signs for each purchase and a paper receipt goes from the merchant to the bank for billing. You are identified by your signature.

In the fully developed EFTS, the plastic card and not the signature has to provide positive identification of the holder of the card. You will not sign anything, so another way has to be found to prevent someone else from using the card. The first thing that is required is a personal identification number along the lines of our Social Insurance Number (SIN). When the federal government first introduced SIN numbers they swore up and down that it was only for a few simple uses such as Family Allowances, Old-Age Pensions, and Income Tax. Now everywhere you turn someone wants your SIN—to get dividends, to open a trust account, to get medical help.

The SIN is the forerunner of the PIN. Every financial transaction where you do not use cash will require your PIN. But can you remember it? No, so you write it down and put it in your wallet along with your plastic card. Your wallet is stolen. The thief has the key to your bank account and cleans it out. The bank is not responsible because you kept your PIN and your card in the same place. But try to think of some way to always have them both with you yet so separate that a thief cannot connect them. How many elderly people can manage that, let alone the rest of us?

Various ways have been suggested to overcome this problem. The cardholder could make a thumb print that is fed into the computer for verification. Or the cardholder could speak into a microphone and have his voice verified by a voice spectrograph.

Because the customer does not sign anything in this system, there is no credit card receipt to be filled out by the merchant. The merchant does not have to send his copy to the bank for processing and the customer does not have his copy for a record. The information is only on magnetic tapes in the computer. What if the computer loses its memory or coughs up the wrong number? You may just be out of luck.

Another feature of the plastic card of the future is its use as both a debit and a credit card. Today's card is either one or the other. A credit card is used to buy something or to borrow money. In either case the bank is providing you with credit. A debit card is used to make deposits and withdrawals from your bank account. There is no credit involved. The funds are transferred immediately from your account to the seller's account.

Several savings and loan associations in the United States introduced these cards in the early 1970s. *Forbes* reported on one of the early uses in 1976:

> The Wilmington (Del.) Savings Fund Society started slowly with a debit card in 1972, which it dubbed WSFS and pronounces WizFiz. By August it will have terminals in 26 supermarkets throughout the state, according to William H. Robinson, senior vice president. A measure of success is being achieved, too, Robinson says, in plans to return to customers each month only a statement without the usual batch of cleared checks—in effect preparing the customer for all-electronic banking. Describing this as "record retention" rather than as "nonreturn of checks," the savings bank has found customers willing to accept the system. But, Robinson emphasized, this requires an unscrambled, descriptive statement with advanced microfilm technology to provide fail-safe proof of payment.[2]

Most bank customers would still consider this "record retention" no matter what new terminology was dreamed up. And it is a major disadvantage because there is no other "fail-safe" proof of payment.

Point-of-Sale Terminals

POSs are placed in stores to provide customers with instant access to their bank accounts through a complicated mechanism of account verification, credit authorization, immediate deduction from a customer's bank account, and immediate addition to the store's account.

You may pay for a television set by presenting a plastic card to the store clerk. The clerk puts the plastic card into the computer terminal in the store. The message travels to the bank's computer, which sorts through its data bank to see if there is enough money in the account to pay for the TV. If there is, the purchase price is immediately taken out of your account. If there is not, the bank computer will tell the POS how much credit you have, extend credit to that amount and record the loan to the bank. The whole transaction is over almost instantaneously. You do not have to go through all the hassle of arranging a loan. The store owner has no cash to count or deposit nor does he have to check out your credit and make out a loan.

Automatic Clearing Houses

The traditional clearing house is a regional organization that receives all the cheques written in that area by creditors, sorts them by bank, and then passes them on to the bank where the cheque writer's deposit is located. Mr. A writes a cheque on his account in the Bank of Montreal and sends it to Mr. B to pay his rent. Mr. B deposits the cheque in his account at the Commerce. The Commerce sends the cheque to the regional clearing centre for sorting. At the end of the day, the clearing house adds up all the cheques and figures out how much money each bank owes the other. If the Commerce owes the Montreal more money than the Montreal owes the Commerce, it settles up the difference.

The process clearly involves a lot of paper shuffling, which the banks want to cut down drastically. That is the rationale for an automatic clearing house which would process pre-authorized payments on magnetic tape in its computer.

An ACH exchanges funds between banks on the basis of data on the magnetic tapes, not on cheques. No paper moves through the system, just a message on a tape giving the payment instructions. This method of transferring money is ideally suited to handling payments that are in fixed amounts and recur on a regular basis such as pensions, family allowances, bond interest, dividends, and mortgage payments. It is a very beneficial system to governments, financial institutions, and large corporations. The advantages are less apparent for the consumer. According to the federal government's huge report by the Canadian Payments System Standards Group chaired by Roger Charbonneau, you will have to learn to like it.

The CPSSG quoted a U.S. survey of consumer attitudes which reported that consumers liked direct deposit because it saved them a trip to the bank, their pay was deposited even when they were away, the bank received the money sooner, there was no risk of forgetting to deposit their pay (!!), and it saved them on postage. (When was the last time you mailed your pay cheque?) In comparison, the survey reported that consumers did not like direct deposit because they lost control of the deposit, their employer might make a mistake, it could be harder to obtain cash, and the bank might make a mistake.

Some difficult individuals said they would refuse to have their pay deposited directly in their bank account because they like to see their pay cheque and handle their own banking. In addition, they did not deposit their entire cheque because they wanted some cash. Another objection was that there were too many errors and delays in the system.

The Charbonneau report brushed these objections aside with the sanguine comment, "Several similar surveys have shown that consumers who are reluctant at first to use a direct payroll deposit service are satisfied with the service once they have been using it for a while. It thus seems that direct deposit of payroll will gradually gain in popularity."[3] That remains to be seen. It certainly will not gain in popularity unless the laws are changed to be sure that individuals are guaranteed the right to consent to or reject direct deposits.

16

How Does EFTS
Affect the Consumer?

EFTS is coming to Canada and it is coming in a legal vacuum, as far as the consumer is concerned. The Ontario government was told this in words that are loud and clear in their specially commissioned report, *The Challenge of EFT: Policy and Legislation Responses*.

According to this report, "The advantages of EFT to banks and near-banks (trust companies, caisses populaires, credit unions, etc.) are obvious—increased speed and efficiency. If these result in lower bank charges, and greater convenience, the customer will gain, too. But EFT, by taking our already-computerized money system a stage further into the electronic future, poses new threats to the customer's privacy, security from deliberate theft, and accidental loss through the muddles and mistakes which are all too frequent in computerized operation. It may turn him into a small, shaky digit, quivering before a colossal unfeeling machine."[1]

Look at this last sentence again. These are not the words of some so-called left-wing consumers' group despised by the Canadian Bankers' Association and the Senate Banking Committee. These are the words of a report that the Ontario government calls "Ontario's contribution to public debate on this issue." It is a fascinating and highly readable report, and frightening. And it comes to the new and very significant conclusion that only on the surface is EFT a matter of banking and telecommunications and therefore to be regulated by the federal government. The real fact is that EFT is "a question of individual privacy, consumer protection and responsibility in business transactions, which should be resolved by the Province, with or without federal initiative.[2]

This viewpoint puts a whole new emphasis and thrust to any attempt at effective consumer legislation in the banking field. The provincial governments are the ones to turn to for real action. There are many problem areas that urgently need attention.

The Chequeless or Minimal-Cheque Society

No cheques is the goal of an EFTS, because it costs $1.4 billion in a year for the Canadian banking system to handle all those pieces of paper. "Had not the Bank of America started automation 25 years ago," commented Herbert J. Richmon, senior vice-president of Data General Corporation, "its present pile of paper work would be higher than its headquarters building in San Francisco and they would be employing more people than General Motors today. The cost of cashing a cheque would be in excess of five dollars a piece." It is no wonder that the banking system wants to eliminate cheques in favour of using magnetic tape.

Consumers are less than enchanted with the prospect; they prefer to have their cheques returned with a monthly statement to prove that they have made the payment, both for their own records and in case of a legal dispute. The banking system will not overcome this justifiable reluctance of consumers to give up cheques until it comes up with an alternate system that provides an easily understandable record that is legally acceptable as proof of payment.

Just how much information is necessary? The consumer's statement must be sufficiently descriptive to prevent the bank or the person to whom the money was or should have been credited from claiming nonpayment against the person who made the payments. That would seem to indicate that the person who made the payment will need a trace number to tie down the transaction, the amount paid, the account number, and the bank to which it was paid.

The person to whom the money is being paid will also need sufficient information to prove that the money was or was not paid to them. There is an added problem here of confidentiality. In some cases, consumers might object to anyone being able to trace payments back to their source.

One of the big problems in checking out errors or disputes is the cost of retrieving the information.

The Bank of Nova Scotia tried to introduce a computer printout in court, according to Gaylen Duncan, executive director of the Canadian Law Information Council in Ottawa, but it took several appeals before a decision was reached that the printout could be introduced provided the bank had detailed descriptions of its internal computer operations. Under these conditions, the cost of a minor error

in a consumer's account makes legal action totally uneconomic. The Ontario report on EFTS says, "At present, disputes over computerized transactions often end in stale-
mate because the expense of retrieving the relevant
information from the innards of the system is greater than
the amount in dispute. The owner of the system should be
obliged to absorb the cost of retrieving evidence from the
system."[3]

You could be a big loser without that protection. Anybody who has found errors in his account and complained
about it can tell you about how long it takes to get an answer. Some people have even been charged interest and
had to fight to get it back, even if the bank finally admitted
it was wrong. Imagine how much worse it will be when
there is no trail of paper to follow.

Float

Under the older and slower system of clearing cheques,
it often took four or five days for a cheque to travel from
the depositor's bank back to the cheque writer's bank. The
depositor was immediately credited with the money but it
was not taken out of the payer's bank account until the
cheque got back there. During this time, the cheque was
said to be "floating."

Consumers liked the float because it gave them five more
days to come up with the money to cover the cheque. Playing the float became a common game for many adroit consumers.

Now faster or even instantaneous transfers in and out of
accounts have almost eliminated the float. Many credit
transfers are made immediately because branches are con-

nected to the central computer. This is called "on-line banking" and it means no waiting for credit transfers. That pleases banks very much because float often amounted to $1.2 billion in Canada and a few customers were abusing it. Now a banking institution takes the money out of a depositor's account and holds it for several days before putting it into the account of the person to whom it is owed. This is the same as a deposit on which no interest is being paid.

The Individual's Right to Consent

With the present banking system, every individual has the right to choose his banking institution. You can use whichever bank, trust company, or credit union you wish to use. No one says that because you work for Company X you must bank at Bank B. For that matter, nobody says you have to go to a bank at all. You can cash your government cheques at the grocery store and keep your cash in the cookie jar. But all that freedom is about to vanish.

In an EFTS, you will have to use the banking system and you may not even be able to choose which bank you use. The government, the company you work for, and the banks will decide that, not you.

Employers will place pressure on employees to use the employer's bank because they are also under pressure to push business into that direction. However, payroll is not the only banking business that the bank does for your employer. The bank also provides your company with essential working capital and long-term loans. It may have bought a sizable amount of a recent bond issue which is paying for the new expansion of the plant that is necessary to keep the company competitive and prosperous. Your company, in other words, is very dependent on the good will of its banker.

The banker, in turn, knows this and can put pressure on the company to direct as much business as possible its way. It would like to do the data processing for the accounts receivable and the payroll. And it would be very convenient if the payroll all went into deposits at that bank instead of deposits at competitor's banks.

Do you see the pressure building up? The company needs the good will of the bank. The bank suggests that the company should lean on its employees to have their deposits at that bank.

Large financial institutions that hold the bank accounts of major corporations or governments will benefit immensely from credit transfers, so they are likely to offer cost incentives and other benefits to get this business. This could result in the major financial institutions taking business away from smaller financial institutions, which would lead to even more concentration of economic power than there is now.

Safeguards must be built into the system to prevent this by ensuring the consumers are free to choose their bank. Consumers also have to be encouraged to overcome their customary apathy by genuinely using their freedom of choice.

The Law Reform Commission points out, "Freedom to choose between financial institutions is in the interest of the non-banks and smaller chartered banks. But no deposit institution has an economic interest in individual freedom to consent to electronic credit transfer, once neutrality between institutions is assured. Even labour and poverty groups, to the extent that deposit institutions embodying their social goals are organized, can be expected to abandon the ideological point. Institutional pressure in favour of genuine consent is likely to decrease. Unless the individual right to 'opt in' is firmly entrenched at an early stage, it is reasonable to predict that 'consent' will soon be proposed as a right to 'opt out.' Students of consumer behaviour know that there is no choice at all. If an individual right to consent to the means of payment is to be imbedded in the law, there will never be more potential support than exists now."[4]

Costs of an EFTS

The standard argument presented by the banking system for introducing an EFTS is to reduce costs, but there is no evidence as yet that computerization has done this. Costs to the consumer have actually been increased. Chequing, safekeeping, loan charges, and almost any other banking service costs more.

The Economic Council of Canada has the situation taped.

> It is generally admitted that significant costs reductions from the introduction of new technology will only be realized over the long-run, and with the exception of its use for cheque clearing, it has not had a large impact on the per unit cost of most of their operations. However, in some instances, it has made it easier for the institutions to shift costs formerly born by them onto the consumer, and to levy direct charges on the ultimate beneficiary of the financial service. The introduction of descriptive billing, for example, has shifted the cost of month-end account verification and reconciliation from the banks to credit card users. Insofar as the latter are not as efficient in providing these services for themselves as are the banks, social costs have increased.[5]

This was not the way it was originally described, of course. Banks claimed that they would save money if there was no float, fewer cheques, and easy credit verification. Costs would be "unbundled," that is, directly traced to each service, and the banks would then know more precisely what to charge for each type of service.

The consumer would then, according to the gospel as spoken by the CBA, benefit by getting more and better service at less cost or at least at a price related closely to cost. The range of services is certainly wider but consumers complain much more about the quality of service and its cost.

During 1978 the price for writing a cheque on a personal chequing account was increased from $.16 to $.18 and charge for package accounts increased from $3.00 to $3.50 a month. At the beginning of 1979, safety deposit boxes went up from $7.50 to $9.00. The excuse for the large percentage increases was that there had been no rate changes during a number of years of high inflation. But during this same period of inflation, the profits of the chartered banks increased even faster. Many of the benefits of the new banking system seem to have gone to the banks, not the consumer.

This is only the start of the EFTS. The future costs will be much greater and they will be borne largely by the users of the system. André Ouellet when he was Minister of Consumer and Corporate Affairs expressed this very view, and he was certainly in a position to know.

At a speech to the Consumer Law Protection Conference in Montreal on September 25, 1975, Ouellet said:

> We know that in Canada we have a highly concentrated financial sector, one in which cost and scale economy considerations will result in few alternative systems, and hence options for the consumer to choose amongst being created. Market forces are

unlikely in and of themselves, therefore, to ensure that consumers will reap the benefits of the new technology.

The Accuracy of an EFTS

One of the touted benefits of EFTS is its purported ability to keep consumers' accounts more accurately. The Bank of Montreal, as an example, printed a pamphlet called *Find Out How Our Bank Computer Improves Service for You,* in which it makes some very strong representations about their accuracy.

> Did you know that the Bank of Montreal's new computer system keeps your bank accounts quickly and accurately up-to-the-minute . . . the system has built-in accuracy. There is less chance of error than with hand operation, because entries are handled fewer times. Every transaction can be verified immediately. Two confirmations are typed simultaneously—one for you and one for branch records. The system improves confidentiality.[6]

Just how accurate is this "built-in accuracy"? It is very difficult, if not impossible, for an outsider to tell. But computer systems do malfunction and bank customers do find errors in their accounts. At present the banks have the upper hand in any dispute.

The only way that there can be a really reliable accuracy is by expensive and repetitive checking of entries and results. The costs of attaining this level of accuracy would be very high and they would likely be passed on to the consumer.

In an analysis of the report to the U. S. Congress of the National Commission on Electronic Fund Transfers, Martin L. Ernst, a vice-president of Arthur D. Little, Inc. said, "Consumer experiences with automated billings give them quite reasonable justification for concern with regard to the difficulties of correcting any mistakes that may have been made."[7]

Fraud is a problem that is even more difficult to deal with than error. It can occur by unauthorized people using your plastic card or by someone manipulating the computer system.

In fact, theft in EFT systems can be committed on a huge scale by anyone who can tap into a central computer operation from a remote terminal, from the central unit itself, or by tapping the wires leading to the central computer. And it is remarkably easy. In April 1980, some kids from Dalton School, a private school in New York, used a portable keyboard and a pay phone to hook into the computer system of GTE Telenet Communications Corporation in Virginia. This data base is linked to Bell Canada's Datapac and this linkage allowed the students to access twenty-one Canadian companies and universities on forty-two occasions, including the universities of Toronto, Alberta, Waterloo, and Concordia as well as the computers of Scott Hart and Associates and Canada Cement. This tampering wiped out 20 percent of Canada Cement's data base.

The most amazing aspect of "computer crimes" like this is that most of them are not really crimes. It is perfectly legal to tell someone about the information in your company's computer or even reveal the access code. We have a long way to go before we reach the Russian attitude to computer crime. According to a report in *B.C. Business,* 64 farm employees deprived the government of $12 million by selling nonexistent vegetables to it, while several truck drivers qualified themselves for bonuses by having a computer report that they had cleared 2 million tons of snow—a quantity that would take twenty years to fall. Five

of the farm workers were, however, shot, and the others received an average sentence of fifteen years.[8]

Some computer thefts are intriguing in their originality.
In a technique known as salami slicing, one computer
junky programmed the big machine to accumulate all the
fractions of cents it dropped when rounding off numbers
and put them into his account. Every time the bank
dropped an amount of less than half a cent when it was
adding interest to a savings account, that fraction of a cent
was stolen by computer theft and credited to the thief's account. In another case a computer consultant, Rifken, stole
$10 million from the Sterling Pacific Bank in California by
telephoning a computer to transfer money to his account in
New York.

An ingenious couple worked out a scheme to transfer
$28 million from Pacific Petroleum's account at the Has-
tings and Seymour branch of the Bank of Nova Scotia to a
branch of the Crocker National Bank in Los Angeles. A
woman called the bank from a street corner phone and
gave code transfer numbers which were supposed to be
confidential. Unfortunately for the thieves, the RCMP were
waiting at the other end of the line. A Vancouver building
materials salesman, Barry Berenbaum, got a three-year
sentence in Los Angeles for theft of $2.8 million.

Computer experts can cite case after case like this where
the increasing complexity of the funds transfer system has
opened the door to bigger and bigger thefts. And despite
denials by the banks, these same computer experts state
without equivocation that the systems are increasing the
potential for "remote mugging." Computer consultant Art
Benjamin is quoted in the *Financial Post* as saying, "A
computer system can't be protected from an expert group
with fraud in mind."[9]

Allan H. MacDonald, president of the Canadian Association for Information Science, says that breaching security codes for any computer system is not hard if a person knows how to go about it. A 1971 report on computers prepared by the Organization for Economic Cooperation and Development says that it is never possible to have perfect security.

For the average consumer, theft may not be as serious a problem as error and malfunction. A computer breakdown can be mildly inconvenient, but it can also be serious, if consumers are denied access to their accounts as a result.

Barbara Sulzenko, Director of Public Policy and Research for the Consumers' Association of Canada testified before the Senate Banking Committee about consumer problems with computers. One example she gave was from her personal experience.

> I might offer a simple example from my own personal experience of where the electronic system has worked to my disadvantage. I bank with a bank which has an electronic system. I went to the bank on Friday afternoon to take some money out of my account to go on a holiday, and I found that the computer was down. It was down for the rest of the afternoon. I had to borrow money on my credit card account. Of course, I incurred costs as a consequence of that borrowing. The bank made no provision to pay back those extra costs that I had incurred because its computer was down. It is because of situations like this that the consumer stands to lose.[10]

Ms. Sulzenko had to pay interest to borrow money because the bank's computer could not print out the amount of money in her bank account. It was solely the fault of the computer system but she had no recourse, although Senator Lang, the Deputy Chairman of the Senate Banking Committee, remarked, "You didn't have to do that. Get a good lawyer."[11] With lawyers charging out their time at $75 an hour, that could be more expensive than borrowing money.

Invasion of Privacy

An EFT system for all of Canada means that there will be one common computer system with a centralized state bank being fed information from every corner of the country. A gold miner in the Yukon could find all the financial facts of his life stored there. So could the longshoreman in Vancouver, the oil rigger in Alberta, and the nurse in Halifax.

It is easy to sound hysterical or paranoid on this subject because for many it conjures up visions of *1984* with the income tax department, the RCMP, the Canadian Bankers' Association, and even organized crime poring over this data for their own mysterious ends. They will know all about your paid (or unpaid) income tax, your nervous breakdown or social disease, your buying habits, and your stock market speculations. It is all there to be retrieved or manipulated by anyone who can get access to the data. Imagine the use that can be made of these facts by unscrupulous governments, employers, tax departments, or bankers. Then remember how easy it is to acquire this information.

An Ontario Royal Commission investigating the confidentiality of health records found that private investigators posing as nurses or doctors over the telephone were able to get secret medical information for employers and insurance companies. There have also been reports of leaked information from government hospital insurance records. The RCMP have gained access to confidential tax information.

Invasion of privacy has been even more alarming in the United States. The FBI examined bank records of antiwar and black-power groups in the late 1960s; the Nixon White House used government files during their war on alleged subversives and "political enemies." Alan F. Westin, a professor of public law and government at Columbia University, says that these disclosures have increased the concern about an EFT system and "civil libertarians have warned that proposals for developing such a 'checkless-cashless society' are extraordinarily dangerous."[12]

But things like that could surely never happen in Canada! Most Canadians think not.

Publicity about these invasions of personal privacy do not seem to have had any real impact on the average Canadian. We are strangely apathetic about the whole business. As a result most governments have been lukewarm or even indifferent to the whole subject of the right to privacy. Some laws have been passed on privacy, confidentiality, and credit reporting, but they do not deal effectively with the individual's right to privacy.

British Columbia, Saskatchewan, and Manitoba passed privacy acts but they all turned out to be ineffective because they need a costly and cumbersome procedure to get results. Laws regulating consumer credit reporting are not really effective either in dealing with possible abuses arising in an EFT system. The problem becomes even more difficult to control when data is stored outside Canada. The data bank for some Canadian mutual funds is in New Jersey. The RCMP and the FBI have interconnections to provide each other with data. Other financial data on individuals is stored in Europe. Looked at from this wide angle, the right to individual privacy becomes an international problem requiring international solutions.

The Ontario report on EFT was particularly concerned with the dangers to personal privacy. "EFT will be a centralized, computerized operation and, as such, a threat to personal privacy."[13] It concluded that controls must be put on the use of EFT data.

The report pointed directly at the banking practice of getting customers to sign blanket waivers of confidentiality when opening deposit accounts, joining a package plan, or borrowing money. The commission believes that if these waiver clauses were made illegal, the banks might show more respect for the privacy of their customers. Without this change, the banks can use their power to force customers into revealing personal information under threat of withholding credit or other banking services.

Westin has a particularly interesting suggestion for protecting the privacy of the individual. He believes that the permanent data base on an individual built up by an EFT system creates a trustee relationship between the banking system and the individual. If this is so, the data profile of the individual held in the system is a legal property that belongs only to the individual and not to the system. The managers of the EFT system should use this information only for the funds transfer process and its necessary monitoring for security purposes. The information must not be used for any other gainful purpose without obtaining the individual's consent and paying him compensation. As an example, banks use it for cross-selling. Your bank sees the size of your pay cheque and will approach you about buying a Registered Retirement Savings Plan. It can even sell the fact that you earn $30,000 and subscribe to *Gourmet* to the direct mailing list of the Fruit-of-the-Month Club without your approval. "The sooner American consumers wake up to the fact that amassed personal facts about them are becoming the necessary currency of marketing in our economy," says Westin, "the sooner we will have a new and more humanistic exchange theory of value for the electronic age."[14]

No matter what legal provisions are introduced, EFTS is bound to change the way we think about money. It will become far less tangible because we will seldom touch it or see it. It will become mostly figures on a page which we juggle like mad bookkeepers.

The concern of many people is that this state of mind may lead us to lose our consciousness of the value of money as many people do when they get a credit card. It could then tempt consumers into inflationary spending patterns and debt loads well beyond their financial capacity.

People who lead a marginal economic existence will also suffer. At present these people have no access to credit cards but some way will have to be found to give them a transaction card because everyone will need one. That can only mean that these people will have to be given a small line of credit and be tied into the banking system. This will lead to acute culture shock for these people unless they are prepared carefully for the cashless society.

EFTS is also affecting the relationship of the average consumer to the whole banking system through the dehumanizing effect of the machine versus man. The expenses of on-line computers and other lead-ins to EFTS are making small branches uneconomic. The Commerce closed three of these branches in small B.C. communities in August 1979. The closing of their Alert Bay branch means that bank customers have to take a ferry to Port McNeil. Larger communities have a different problem. In many cases, there are more branch offices than necessary so banks are consolidating their facilities into bigger and bigger branches. This can only increase the remoteness of the average consumer from any human contact.

A letter in *Business Week* brought this problem into sharp focus.

People vs. computers

Your article on "Consumer banking: Why everybody wants a piece of the business" (Money & banking, Apr. 23) mentioned "changing technology and delivery systems." Commercial banks are showing considerable ingenuity in trying to attract more business, but along the way many of them are forgetting that banking essentially is a people-to-people relationship. The frenetic rush to computerize services is dehumanizing the relationships with customers. Several years ago, during a consulting assignment for one of the leading commercial banks seeking to build its retail business, in answer to one of our questions about future objectives, a top executive answered: "My fond hope is that one day we shall never have to deal with people . . . the machines will do that." The bank is nearing its questionable goal; computers are taking over.

Banks have yet to learn how to "balance" people and machines. In answer to criticism, some banks claim that they actually employ more people than ever before. Apparently they need more people to handle the complaints from customers . . . complaints caused by malfunctioning computers.[15]

CONCLUSION

Don't Bank on It

The banking system is changing our economic and social life. It is changing the way we handle money, the way we think about money, and the control we have over our economic lives. It is doing all this with government support. And it is doing it in the spirit of Big Brother knows what is best for us all.

No other major industry is allowed to operate with such disdain for the consumer and yet probably no other industry is as important to the average person. Steel mills are no longer allowed to belch black smoke into a community. Mining smelters must control their poisonous fumes. Pulp mills cannot discharge mercury into fishing streams. Car manufacturers must install seat belts and control fuel emissions. Land developers have to plan their projects around the community's standards and wishes.

In sharp contrast, the banking industry appears to believe that it has the right to flaunt provincial laws, to deceive its customers, and to withhold vital information. The consumer of these services can be cajoled, manipulated, cheated, or defrauded by the banking system but apparently no laws or regulations or supervisory bodies should be introduced to protect the consumer. And to make matters worse, the federal government seems to support the banks—at least it does next to nothing to stop this kind of behaviour.

Canadian consumers have the banking system that the federal government wants and the federal government has shaped and manipulated the banking system to serve its own purposes. Despite all the rhetoric about competition, it is a banking system where the power is concentrated in a few hands. The most important decisions can be made by a few people in a few minutes if necessary.

This suits the federal government perfectly. The banking system is one of the most important avenues for the government to carry out its economic policy. It would be possible to carry out this policy through the banking system by means of laws and regulations as many countries do, and the Canadian banking system does have a framework of such laws and regulations. But the real control of the Canadian banking system is carried out by something elegantly called "moral suasion." The Minister of Finance or the Governor of the Bank of Canada has a quiet chat with the presidents of the five largest banks and—lo and behold —we have a new economic policy in place. Certainly beats having to talk to the presidents of 1,400 banks, as he might have to do in the U.S.A.

This all makes for a very chummy relationship between the federal government and the largest banks. It may even explain the comment of Allen Lambert, the former president of Toronto-Dominion, when the government released its proposals for the next Bank Act. "There were not many surprises," he said. "The paper followed fairly closely the recommendations of the Canadian Bankers' Association."[1]

This is certainly as good an explanation as any for all the plums thrown the way of the chartered banks. First the banks sought easy access to consumer lending and they quickly swept that market. They also sought easy access to the mortgage market and they are now well on their way to a big slice of that pie. Next on the banks' agenda is selling securities, giving investment advice, doing their customers' data processing, and controlling the leasing market.

This concentration of power is peanuts, however, compared to what will happen in the future when the federal government imposes an electronic funds transfer system on the docile consumers of Canada. This system, I have shown, is being carefully designed and crafted to centralize power without any legal safeguards for consumers.

The federal government can do this because it controls banking and interest rates by virtue of the powers given it by the British North America Act. It can do this because banking legislation is written by the powerful Department of Finance and the Bank of Canada. It can do this because federal governments have done everything in their power to weaken the Department of Consumer and Corporate Affairs and make certain it has no influence on any changes in banking legislation.

Like it or not we have entered the brave new world of the electronic funds transfer where everybody must be tied into the system. The federal government has been actively promoting this society for many years, ostensibly on the grounds that it will be a more efficient way to handle payments in the economy and will increase the effectiveness of monetary policy. It is also a great help when the post office goes on strike. But EFTS implies a great deal more than that. Because it produces huge banks of data on every economic transaction that a consumer makes, it allows anyone with access to that data to know a great deal about others'

266

ConclusionConclusion

lives, more even than you care to have known. It would be of enormous interest to the tax department, the RCMP, the banking system, and organized crime.

Nothing is being built into this EFTS to ensure that consumers have a genuine right to privacy, that computer errors or fraud will be settled quickly and fairly, or that everyone has the right to consent to their participation. The Canadian Bankers' Association takes the view that these concerns are not really valid and there is nothing to worry about.

In a publication called *The Chartered Banks of Canada 1978–79*, the CBA claims, "The emergence of new technology has led to considerable comment on the concept of electronic funds transfer system (EFTS), some of it ill-informed. There has been some public concern that the new method for moving funds would adversely affect the customer's traditional right of full control over the disbursement of his or her own deposits and the privacy of records. . . . Such concerns are groundless. Moreover, concern that the cashless, chequeless society is imminent, or indeed that it will ever take over entirely, is also groundless."[2]

The Economic Council of Canada shoots these arguments down completely. "The movement towards an electronics payments mechanism," according to the Council, "is now well underway and appears irreversible." The Council also believes, "Planning a national electronic funds transfer system requires the resolution of many complex issues which relate to competition, government regulation, concentration of economic power and public participation. This will not be easy, especially since it involves all levels of government and a wide cross-section of industries."[3]

Yet people in positions of great economic or political power do not appear able to grasp the significance of these new economic trends. This type of attitude was very apparent when the Consumers' Association of Canada presented its brief on the revision of the Bank Act to the influential Senate Banking, Trade and Finance Committee.

The Consumers' Association believes quite rightly that there should be consumer representation on the Canadian Payments Association when it is planning the introduction of EFTS. The chairman of the Banking Committee, Senator Salter Hayden, acted as though it was the most outrageous idea he had ever heard. As quoted in *Hansard*, the 84-year-old corporate lawyer commented to the Consumers' Association, "And you want to be in on that, the consumer?"[4]

There is only one aspect of the federal scene that does seem to be making a small, tentative move towards helping the consumer. The office of the Inspector General of Banks is taking increasing notice of consumer problems, even though this is not normally considered a function of that office. Its main concern, according to the Bank Act, is to protect the solvency of the banking's system through regular and thorough inspections. The Bank Act does not, according to Inspector General W. A. Kennett, give him the power to ask a bank to behave. He can only use his "moral suasion," which is considerable.

Any intervention by the Inspector General into banking practices which consumers protest is really at his pleasure. He has no mandate to protect the consumer apart from reporting on the financial solvency of the bank.

The complaints that he receives are along the lines of the ones you have already read about: the Rule of 78, delays in banks crediting payments, the low interest paid on tax accounts held for mortgage borrowers, the right of set-off for debts due on credit cards, problems with defective merchandise bought on credit cards, continual increases in credit limits for no good reason, billing errors on credit cards and the long time taken to correct them, no daily interest, and refusal to show an appraisal report even though the customer paid for it.

The Bank Act is startlingly negligent in consumer protection. "There is no provision for the Inspector General of Banks to inquire into any hanky panky, by any of the banks," Bob Briscoe, the M.P. for Kootenay-West, told the House of Commons. "There is no slap on the wrist, no investigation. The bank is supposed to examine itself and make sure it did right by its client."⁵

The federal government obviously does not care or, even more likely, prefers to cater to the wishes of the banks and keep the power structure heading the way it is going—toward more and more power for the banking system. Barring some radical change of heart, the only hope for consumers lies in their provincial governments. But even here it is difficult to be very optimistic.

The former Minister of Consumer and Corporate Affairs in British Columbia, Rafe Mair, was leading a very effective attack on the banks for breaking provincial laws in ways which would not be tolerated in less influential organizations when he was removed from his job and replaced by a minister who is either indifferent to the subject or opposed to it. He is keeping so quiet it is hard to tell.

What this all boils down to is that nobody in Canada has the power to say to the banks, "Cut that out!" Sure, you can take them to court if you have lots of money and can get a lawyer equal to the big guns who work for the banks. But that is clearly out of the question for the average consumer. "Theoretically, they are subject to prosecution in both criminal and civil courts," says Paul Raugust of the Vancouver *Sun,* "but in practice the public has virtually no way to challenge banks on their behaviour, ethics or even when they are breaking the Bank Act."[6]

David W. Green in his hard-hitting critique of our banking system says, "The Canadian authorities have acknowledged that the Canadian banks are so powerful that their activities cannot be allowed totally free rein without extreme difficulty for other institutions." He then goes on to point out some of the reasons: the sheer size of Canadian banks, their extensive branch network, the resulting economies from a large operation, and the convenience for a consumer of having a department store of banking for all his needs. Green then sums up his view of bank power with an apt story told him by a friend, who claimed that the vice-president of a U.S. bank once said, "Let's face it, we are in a poker game, and the banks have been dealt four aces. They are concentration, availability, customer trust and price. We would be irresponsible businessmen if we didn't play our hand to the full."[7]

And the banks have played their hand very adroitly. They are masters of manipulating consumers. Look at the red convertible loans; the money you never knew you had. Canadian consumers now spend 42 percent of their income to pay off debts of various kinds. Does anybody honestly think they got in that state without a lot of urging and pushing by those friendly people who loan you money?

The problem, as I have repeatedly said, will get much worse when Canada has a real electronic funds transfer system. Then the banking system will have almost unlimited scope for manipulating consumers through their data banks and control of all financial payments. Unfortunately for consumers this is the kind of situation with which consumers are least capable of dealing. The home economics type of consumer can deal fairly effectively with a coffee pot that falls apart; he or she cannot deal effectively with very complex issues like the right to opt out of an EFT system or legal issues like the rights of a buyer of defective merchandise when payment is made by a bank credit card. The old slogan *"caveat emptor,"* or buyer beware, is not good enough.

There must be a switch to *caveat venditor*—let the seller beware—which makes sellers subject to social forces and values backed up by government regulations. It is also hoped that the sellers will develop greater social responsibility.

President John Kennedy in his consumer message to Congress in 1962 said that consumers have four basic rights. They have a right to safety. They have a right to be informed, which means protection against fraudulent, deceitful, or grossly misleading information or advertising. Consumers also have the right to choose so they are assured access to a variety of products and services at competitive prices. Finally, consumers have the right to be heard. They should be assured that consumer interests will receive full and sympathetic consideration when the government is formulating policy and a fair treatment in its administrative tribunals.

Put these "basic consumer rights" into the Canadian context and the only right that Canadian consumers have with the banking system is safety. As far as the rest is concerned, it is every consumer for himself. Warren Almand, the former Minister of Consumer and Corporate Affairs, has said that consumers will get less protection from government from now on and they have only themselves to blame. "Consumers have been outhustled by business: while business has been lobbying over new consumer legislation, consumers have done nothing."[8] When the government presented the Borrowers' and Depositors' Protection

Bill, the government had strong representations by business but they had virtually no representatives from either consumer groups or other political parties. There was not one question in the House of Commons about when the government was going to reintroduce the bill. The government then dropped the BDP bill and brought in an alternative Credit and Savings Bill that was much more favourable to the banking system.

Almand's allegations of lack of consumer support are not correct. The Consumers' Association of Canada spoke to him on many occasions about the bill and made several presentations to parliamentary committees. But the CAC had to buck some formidable opposition. "As has happened so often before," commented Jacob Ziegel, a law professor at the University of Toronto and chairman of the CAC committee which examined the Borrowers' and Depositors' Protection Bill, "we found ourselves seriously handicapped by a lack of resources. The bill is a highly technical and complex one, which requires much more detail and expert study than the volunteer committee established by CAC was in a position to give."[9]

As Howard Eddy, a consultant to the Law Reform Commission, one of the most informed and rational commentators on this subject, said several years ago, "It is time that we talked about EFTS as if people really mattered." In a speech at the annual meeting of the B.C. Central Credit Union in June 1977, Eddy also commented, "We should reject a system in which people serve things, corporations and governments. That kind of system is built the wrong way around and I for one would wish no part of it. But if our priorities are in the right place, if we seek to make the system truly responsive to the needs of the consumer, the small businessman and the farm proprietor, perhaps we can gain at reasonable cost the benefits in planning, accounting and efficiency which large corporations have been able to buy because they are large corporations. That kind of people-oriented system is one in which we all could happily participate."

How do we go about achieving this? One extreme view is that we should nationalize the banks. Buy them up or expropriate them with tax dollars. After all, government now guarantees the solvency of the banks. One European study of this possibility questioned "whether the development of giant banks and the concentration of banking business have not brought us to a point where nationalization of banks would not make much difference to the functioning of the system, while implying a maximum guaranty to lenders and borrowers."[10]

Nationalized banks are common in many parts of the world. What they would accomplish in Canada is difficult to tell. The more likely development in Canada is towards provincial banks. These financial institutions have a long history going back to the 1830s when savings banks were formed by the governments of Nova Scotia and Newfoundland. Alberta still has its Treasury Branches and Ontario has its Savings Offices. B.C. flirted recently with the idea of the British Columbia Savings and Trust Corporation. None of these have been really successful, which seems to indicate the Canadians prefer to have their banking institutions out of the hands of the government.

That leaves only one alternative. Canadians must have more say and influence in the planning and operation of the banking system. The CAC presented a very sound case for consumer representation of the Canadian Payments Association. Canadians also need a Division of Consumer Affairs attached to the Bank of Canada modelled after a similar division attached to the Federal Reserve System in the United States.

This Federal Division of Consumer Affairs has a Consumer Advisory Council that was formed in 1976 to advise and consult with the Federal Reserve Board. It also has a compliance section which is responsible for the education of consumer credit protection examiners and reviews their reports. It began by identifying several areas of potential problems and supplied the examiners with a questionnaire that is used during the examination of banks to check for unfair and deceptive acts or practices by banks. The questionnaire was so successful in detecting problems that the Federal Deposit Insurance Corporation and the Comptroller of the Currency began using it in 1978 to find out the prevalence and the significance of these practices among the banks that they supervised. The board also developed a computerized program to identify the common types of violators, their geographical concentration, and any other patterns which might help to locate others. It is this kind of initiative and research which is so sadly lacking in Canada.

The root of this problem is the federal government's obsession with banking as an essential element of government policy and the bankers' obsession with banking as a business like any other. It is not. Consumers know this because banking impinges on everyone's economic life. If bankers do not realize this, they should read their own bible a little more carefully. An article called "Social Responsibility in Banking" written by an American, Dr. Peter S. Rose, looked at recent social legislation in the United States which was having profound and disturbing influences on American bankers.

"Banks and bankers are not separate from the communities they serve," says Rose. "Rather, both are an integral part of the economic and social fabric which binds the community's economic character and growth and even its social make-up. At times bankers see their institutions as completely independent of the great social issues of modern-day society—racial equality, social justice, better housing and education, consumer protection, and economic freedom. However, like it or not, what the banker does and how well he does it matters greatly in the social arena."[11]

Until the banking industry recognizes this and the federal government stops bowing to their powerful lobbies, the consumer will always be low man on the totem pole. The only option is to be knowledgeable and aware of how the banking system operates, and support any valid organization or political body working to achieve a more responsible banking system.

NOTES

INTRODUCTION

1. Vancouver *Sun,* April 2, 1980, p. B3.
2. Toronto *Globe and Mail,* October 23, 1980, p. 10.

CHAPTER 2

1. *Report of the Royal Commission on Corporate Concentration* (Supply and Services Canada, March 1978), p. 248.
2. Vancouver *Sun,* May 8, 1978, p. 8.
3. *Report of the Royal Commission on Corporate Concentration, op. cit.,* p. 219.
4. *Corporate Concentration and Banking in Canada,* The Bank of Nova Scotia, February 1976, p. 3.
5. Roy A. Schotland, "Conflicts of Interest Within the Financial Firm: Regulatory Implications," in *Issues in Financial Regulation,* ed. Franklin R. Edwards (New York: McGraw-Hill, 1979), p. 144.

CHAPTER 3

1. Peter C. Newman, *The Canadian Establishment* (Toronto: McClelland and Stewart, 1975), p. 105.
2. Susan Peterson, *Canadian Directorship Practices: A Critical Self-Examination,* The Conference Board in Canada, 1977, p. 154.
3. *Report of the Royal Commission on Corporate Concentration, op. cit.,* p. 254.

4. Newman, p. 90.

5. Roy Baldwin and Leonard Waverman, *Report to the Department of Consumer and Corporate Affairs on the Interlocking Directorates Among the Largest 260 Corporations in Canada* (Institute for the Quantitative Analysis of Social and Economic Policy, University of Toronto, 1971), p. 56.

6. Allan Fotheringham, "Why Keeping Your Money in an Old Sock Is an Increasingly Better Idea," *Maclean's Magazine*, January 23, 1978, p. 64.

7. Louis D. Brandeis, "The Endless Chain," *Harper's Weekly*, December 6, 1913, p. 13.

8. *Investigation of Concentration of Control of Money and Credit*, House of Representatives, No. 1593, February 28, 1913.

9. *Staff Report to the Antitrust Subcommittee of the Committee on the Judiciary*, House of Representatives, March 12, 1965.

10. *Report of the Royal Commission on Corporate Concentration*, *op. cit.*, p. 255.

11. John Kenneth Galbraith, *The New Industrial State* (Boston: Houghton Mifflin, 1967).

12. Toronto *Globe and Mail*, July 25, 1977, p. B6.

13. *The Canadian Banker and ICB Review*, Vol. LXXXVI (April 1979), p. 7.

14. John Porter, *The Vertical Mosaic* (University of Toronto Press, 1965), p. 255.

15. Toronto *Globe and Mail*, May 5, 1979, p. B6.

CHAPTER 4

1. Sir John Hicks, *Critical Essays in Monetary Policy* (Oxford University Press, 1967), p. 59.

2. Stephen R. Malin, "Money-Watching," *Across the Board, The Conference Board Magazine*, September 1980, p. 61.

3. *Report of the Royal Commission on Banking and Finance* (Queen's Printer, 1964), pp. 95–96.

4. Toronto *Globe and Mail*, June 24, 1978, p. B1.

CHAPTER 5

1. *Report of the Royal Commission on Corporate Concentration*, *op. cit.*, p. 229.

CHAPTER 6

1. Hugh Anderson, Toronto *Globe and Mail,* June 23, 1979, p. 83.
2. William K. Brandt and George S. Pey, "International Disclosure and Consumer Behaviour: An Empirical Evaluation of Truth in Lending," *Journal of Law Reform,* 1974.
3. Federal Reserve Board, *Annual Report* (Washington, D.C., 1977), p. 34.

CHAPTER 7

1. Anthony Whittingham, "What A Tangled Web We Weave," *Maclean's Magazine,* August 4, 1980, p. 30.
2. Alix Granger, "The Regulation of Trust Companies and Finance Companies in British Columbia," (Master's Thesis, Simon Fraser University, 1968).

CHAPTER 8

1. The Law Reform Commission of Canada, *The Cheque,* (Supply and Sources Canada, 1979), p. 5.
2. Vancouver *Express,* June 11, 1979, p. A13.
3. *Consumer Reports,* January 1975, p. 35.
4. Toronto *Globe and Mail,* November 28, 1978, p. 1.
5. Vancouver *Express,* June 11, 1979, p. A13.
6. Vancouver *Sun,* March 29, 1978, p. D8.
7. Vancouver *Province,* August 12, 1978.
8. Howard R. Eddy, *The Canadian Payment System and the Computer: Issue for Law Reform* (Ottawa: Law Reform Commission, 1974), p. 24.
9. *Consumer Reports,* January 1975, p. 34.

CHAPTER 9

1. Vancouver *Sun,* January 16, 1980, p. 1.
2. Consumers' Association of Canada, *Addendum to Submission to the Senate Committee on Banking, Trade and Commerce Concerning the 1979 Bank Act Revisions,* p. 2.

CHAPTER 10

1. Stephen Leacock, *Literary Lapses* (Toronto: McClelland and Stewart, 1910), p. 1.
2. Vancouver *Sun,* July 21, 1979, p. B8.
3. Allan A. Parker, *Credit Law and Bankruptcy Handbook* (Vancouver: International Self-Counsel Press, 1979), p. 4.
4. Vancouver *Province,* April 12, 1978, p. B7.
5. Fotheringham, *op. cit.,* p. 64.
6. Consumers' Association of Canada, *op. cit.,* p. 2.
7. *The Bank Act,* Burns Fry Limited, July 30, 1980, p. 5.
8. Vancouver *Sun,* March 21, 1978, p. 1.
9. *Ibid.,* p. A10.
10. Vancouver *Province,* October 23, 1978, p. C1.

CHAPTER 11

1. *The Canadian Banker and ICB Review,* April 1979, p. 9.
2. *Bank Act 77: As Others See Us,* The Canadian Bankers' Association, p. 20.
3. *The Financial Post,* June 30, 1979, p. W2.
4. *North Shore News,* June 3, 1980, p. 56.
5. *The Financial Post,* October 21, 1978, p. 12.
6. *North Shore News,* April 8, 1979, p. 65.
7. *Forbes,* August 1, 1971, p. 58.

CHAPTER 12

1. *The Financial Times,* April 12, 1978, p. 1.
2. Howard R. Eddy, *The Canadian Payment System and the Computer: Issue for Law Reform* (Ottawa: Law Reform Commission, 1974).
3. Linda McFennel and Robert H. Long, *Payment Services* (Park Ridge, Ill.: Bank Administration Institute, 1972).
4. *Consumer Reports,* March 1975, p. 174.
5. H. H. Binhammer and Jane Williams, *Deposit-Taking Institutions: Innovation and the Process of Change,* Economic Council of Canada, 1976, p. 109.
6. McFennel and Long, *op. cit.*
7. *Forbes,* May 15, 1976, p. 58.

8. The Consumers' Association of Canada: *Submission to the Standing Committee on Health, Welfare and Social Affairs on Bill C-16*, March 1977, p. 3.
9. *Ibid.*, p. 29.
10. Vancouver *Province*, June 1, 1978, p. 25.
11. Martin J. Meyer, *Credit-Cardsmanship: How to Survive the Credit Card Nightmare and Turn Plastic into Gold* (Lynbrook, N.Y.: Farnsworth Publishing, 1971), p. 121.
12. *Chargex Bulletin*, Summer 1975.
13. *Efficiency and Regulation: A Study of Deposit Institutions*, Economic Council of Canada, 1976, p. 110.
14. *Ibid.*, p. 11.
15. *Ibid.*, p. 14.
16. *Consumer Reports*, March 1975, p. 175.
17. *Wall Street Journal*, July 3, 1979, p. 1.
18. Thomas Russell, *The Economics of Bank Credit Cards* (New York: Praeger, 1975), p. 100.

CHAPTER 15

1. Binhammer and Williams, *op. cit.*, p. 123.
2. *Forbes,* July 1, 1976, p. 70.
3. Canadian Payments System Standards Group, *Final Report*, July 1978, p. 116.

CHAPTER 16

1. *The Challenge of EFT: Policy and Legislation Responses to Electronic Funds Transfer,* commissioned by the government of Ontario, December 1978, p. 2.
2. *Ibid.*, p. 3.
3. *Ibid.*, p. 5.
4. *Payment by Credit Transfer*, Law Reform Commission of Canada, 1978, pp. 9–12.
5. Binhammer and Williams, p. 143.
6. *Find Out How Our Bank Computer Improves Service for You,* Bank of Montreal.
7. Martin L. Ernst, "Electric Funds Transfer: Too Much Too Soon, *IEEE Spectrum,* May 1977, p. 55.
8. *B.C. Business,* October 1980, p. 93.
9. *Financial Post,* May 19, 1979, p. F5.

10. Senate of Canada, Standing Senate Committee on Banking, Trade and Commerce, February 7, 1979, pp. 22–24.
11. *Ibid.,* p. 12.
12. Alan F. Westin, *Privacy Aspects in EFT Systems, Issues in Financial Regulation* (New York: McGraw-Hill, 1979), p. 301.
13. *The Challenge of EFT,* p. 12.
14. Westin, p. 305.
15. *Business Week,* May 28, 1979, p. 7.

CONCLUSION

1. Fotheringham, *op. cit.*
2. The Canadian Bankers' Association, *The Chartered Banks of Canada 1978–79,* p. 9.
3. Binhammer and Williams, *op. cit.,* p. 145.
4. *Hansard,* February 28, 1978, p. 43.
5. The Senate of Canada, *Proceedings of the Standing Committee on Banking, Trade and Commerce,* February 7, 1979.
6. Vancouver *Sun,* March 25, 1978, p. C5.
7. David W. Green, *The Canadian Financial System Since 1965: Competition and Structural Change* (Cardiff: Bangor Occasional Papers in Economics, University of Wales Press, 1974), p. 50.
8. Vancouver *Sun,* May 26, 1978, p. A1.
9. Vancouver *Sun,* May 31, 1978, p. B3.
10. *La Banque dans le Monde de Demain* (Institut Universitaire International Luxembourg, 1975), p. 35.
11. Peter S. Rose, "Social Responsibility in Banking: Part I," *The Canadian Banker and ICB Review,* Vol. 86, No. 2 (April 1979), p. 62.

INDEX

Vice-president of a Vancouver investment dealer, Alix Granger is also the author of *Trusts and Trust Companies in Canada*. She holds a Masters degree in economics (specializing in financial institutions) and teaches courses in investments and personal financial management at the University of British Columbia.